SALLY BURKE

CYNDIE CLAYPOOL DE NEVE

start with praise

HARVEST HOUSE PUBLISHERS
EUGENE, OREGON

Cyndie de Neve is published in association with William K. Jensen Literary Agency, 119 Bampton Court, Eugene, Oregon 97404.

Sally Burke is published in association with William K. Jensen Literary Agency, 119 Bampton Court, Eugene, Oregon 97404.

Cover by Emily Weigel Design

Cover photos © Bashutskyy / Shutterstock

Start with Praise
Copyright © 2018 Sally Burke and Cyndie Claypool de Neve
Published by Harvest House Publishers
Eugene, Oregon 97408
www.harvesthousepublishers.com

ISBN 978-0-7369-7169-0 (pbk)
ISBN 978-0-7369-7170-6 (eBook)

Library of Congress Cataloging-in-Publication Data is on file at the Library of Congress, Washington, DC.

Printed in the United States of America

18 19 20 21 22 23 24 25 26 / VP-SK / 10 9 8 7 6 5 4 3 2 1

This devotional is dedicated to every mom around the world who carves out an hour a week to pray in a Moms in Prayer group. Oh, how God is using your prayers to impact children and schools!

Contents

Empowered Through Thanksgiving

Empowered Through Intercession

A Scripture Prayer for You from Sally and Cyndie

May the LORD answer you when you are in distress;
may the name of the God of Jacob protect you.
May he send you help from the sanctuary
and grant you support from Zion.
May he remember all your sacrifices
and accept your burnt offerings.
May he give you the desire of your heart
and make all your plans succeed.
May we shout for joy over your victory
and lift up our banners in the name of our God.

May the LORD grant all your requests.

Now this I know:
The LORD gives victory to his anointed.
He answers him from his heavenly sanctuary
with the victorious power of his right hand.
Some trust in chariots and some in horses,
but we trust in the name of the LORD our God.
They are brought to their knees and fall,
but we rise up and stand firm.
LORD, give victory to the king!
Answer us when we call!

PSALM 20 NIV

Let's Get Started... Living Empowered

I pray that the eyes of your heart may be enlightened in order that you may know the hope to which he has called you, the riches of his glorious inheritance in his holy people, and his incomparably great power for us who believe. That power is the same as the mighty strength he exerted when he raised Christ from the dead and seated him at his right hand in the heavenly realms.

EPHESIANS 1:18-20 NIV

The same power that raised Christ from the dead and defeated sin and death is at work within every Christian to empower us to fulfill God's great calling in our lives. Our prayer is that these 40 devotionals, based on the four steps of prayer, will help you live empowered and victorious through the Holy Spirit, so that you can "throw off everything that hinders and the sin that so easily entangles. And let us run with perseverance the race marked out for us, fixing our eyes on Jesus" (Hebrews 12:1-2 NIV).

Christ fulfilled His calling here on earth, and now He lives in each person who has accepted His free gift of salvation. Christ is just as determined and "able to do immeasurably more than all we ask or imagine, according to His power that is at work within us" (Ephesians 3:20 NIV). But one thing can stop Him from accomplishing His will in our lives: ourselves.

We want to help you unlock God's power in your life to do His will for His glory and purpose. Even when Christ was on earth giving His disciples a lesson on prayer, He prayed "Your kingdom come, your will

9

be done" (Matthew 6:10 NIV). Prayer empowers us to do God's will "on earth as it is in heaven."

Do you feel inadequate for the tasks God has set before you, whether it be as an employee, volunteer, student, parent, or caretaker? Remember who Christ chose when He was here on Earth: twelve ordinary men. It was their faith in Christ that set them apart. As Jesus was ascending to heaven, He told them they would soon receive the Holy Spirit and be "clothed with power from on high" (Luke 24:49 NIV). That is the same Holy Spirit that lives in each one of us who has accepted Christ as our personal savior. As Philippians 4:13 reminds us, we don't have to do anything in our own power: "I can do all this through him who gives me strength" (NIV).

• •

Unlock God's power in your life to do
His will for His glory and purpose.

• •

This 40-day devotional is designed to remind you each day what a powerful God we serve. We structured this around the four steps of prayer: 10 devotionals about praising our heavenly Father; 10 devotionals about the peace and power that comes through confessing our daily sins; 10 devotionals about the power in giving thanks, even when it's difficult; and 10 devotionals about interceding with powerful prayers for others, handing every concern to the Lord in prayer.

While we highlight praise, confession, thanksgiving, and intercession separately, each day offers an opportunity to pray through the four steps of prayer, including scripture prayers. During intercession, you will have the opportunity to boldly pray God's Word for your loved ones by placing their names in the scripture prayer. In addition, we've added a section called "petition" where you can pray the scripture prayer for yourself, as well.

Our prayer is that this devotional will encourage God's peace and power to flow through you freely so that you can share the love of Christ with all those around you.

We pray this for you from Ephesians 3.

For this reason I kneel before the Father, from whom every family in heaven and on earth derives its name. I pray that out of his glorious riches he may strengthen you with power through his Spirit in your inner being, so that Christ may dwell in your hearts through faith. And I pray that you, being rooted and established in love, may have power, together with all the Lord's holy people, to grasp how wide and long and high and deep is the love of Christ, and to know this love that surpasses knowledge—that you may be filled to the measure of all the fullness of God.

Now to him who is able to do immeasurably more than all we ask or imagine, according to his power that is at work within us, to him be glory in the church and in Christ Jesus throughout all generations, for ever and ever! Amen.

EPHESIANS 3:14-21 NIV

Empowered Through Praise

As we pray the four steps of prayer, we always start with praise for God's characteristics and attributes. Praise acknowledges God for who He is according to the Scriptures. As we begin by praising our Savior, we are reminded of His mercy and power over sin. There is no sin too big for Him to forgive, and there is no request that He can't answer in His perfect timing and according to His perfect will. As we come to know Him through praise, we grow in the Lord, in His strength, in His power, in His love, and in His peace. We become more Christlike, allowing God to empower us to accomplish His mighty purpose.

Let all that I am praise the Lord;
with my whole heart, I will praise his holy name.

Psalm 103:1 nlt

God enters the praises of His people, and the enemy flees!

1

First Things First: We Start with Praise

· · · · · · · · · · · · · · · · · Cyndie · · · · · · · · · · · · · · · · · ·

I will exalt you, my God and King,
and praise your name forever and ever.
I will praise you every day;
yes, I will praise you forever.
Great is the LORD! He is most worthy of praise!
No one can measure his greatness.

Let each generation tell its children of your mighty acts;
let them proclaim your power.
I will meditate on your majestic, glorious splendor
and your wonderful miracles.
Your awe-inspiring deeds will be on every tongue;
I will proclaim your greatness.
Everyone will share the story of your wonderful goodness;
they will sing with joy about your righteousness.

The LORD is merciful and compassionate,
slow to get angry and filled with unfailing love...

The LORD is righteous in everything he does;
he is filled with kindness.
The LORD is close to all who call on him,
yes, to all who call on him in truth.
He grants the desires of those who fear him;
he hears their cries for help and rescues them.

PSALM 145:1-8; 17-19 NLT

*H*ow do you define a prayer? Is it a quick plea as you dash into an important meeting? Or maybe it's a deal you try to make with the Lord when money is tight—something like "Lord, if You help us make our rent this month, then I'll be sure to attend church this weekend." Or maybe you've given up praying all together, because You think God's just too busy to be bothered with the likes of you. Maybe you assume God has so many bigger issues that He couldn't possibly care enough to answer your prayers.

Yet the Bible commands us to bring all our concerns to the Lord in prayer. Philippians 4:6-7 says, "Don't worry about anything; instead, pray about everything. Tell God what you need, and thank him for all he has done. Then you will experience God's peace, which exceeds anything we can understand. His peace will guard your hearts and minds as you live in Christ Jesus" (NLT).

The amazing fact about prayer is that God *wants* us to call on Him. He wants us to spend time with Him. He wants us to develop our love relationship with Him. But how fun is it to always spend time with someone who just asks for this and asks for that? That's one of the reasons that we start the Moms in Prayer group times by praising the Lord. Through praise we get to know who our heavenly Father is—His character, His names, His attributes. When we come to the Lord with a big concern, and start with praise, we remind ourselves that no problem is too big for the ultimate Problem Solver.

Did you know we are commanded to praise the Lord? Look back through Psalm 145. It doesn't say, *you probably should praise the Lord occasionally, when you think about it.* No, Psalm 103:22 says, "Praise the LORD, everything he has created, everything in all his kingdom. Let all that I am praise the LORD" (NIV).

· ·

Through praise we get to know
who our heavenly Father is—His
character, His names, His attributes.

· ·

Starting with praise helps us follow the command in Colossians 3:2 which says, "Set your minds on things above, not on earthly things" (NIV). When we begin to set our minds on God in heaven and not on our problems on earth, we become more confident in Christ and peace-filled, knowing that no matter what happens, we are promised in Romans 8:28 that "God causes everything to work together for the good of those who love God and are called according to his purpose for them" (NLT).

· · · · · · · · · · · · · · · · · Praise · · · · · · · · · · · · · · · · ·

Lord, You truly are "most worthy of praise" as is written in Psalm 145. You are merciful and compassionate, slow to get angry, and filled with unfailing love. Oh, Lord, we do not deserve Your mercy, love, or compassion; yet You freely offer it to us because we are Your children and You love us. How we praise You for Your free gift of undeserved love.

· · · · · · · · · · · · · · · · Confession · · · · · · · · · · · · · · · ·

Lord, You always deserve praise, yet I don't always remember to praise You. Often I focus so much on my fear and worry that I fail to follow Your wisdom to set my mind "on things above, not on earthly things" (Colossians 3:2 NIV). Lord, please forgive me for not moving my eyes from the problem onto You, the only true Problem Solver.

· · · · · · · · · · · · · · · Thanksgiving · · · · · · · · · · · · · · · ·

"You satisfy the hunger and thirst of every living thing" (Psalm 145:16 NLT). Lord, I thank You for providing for me and my family. For every meal that I might take for granted, thank You! Specifically, Lord, I thank You for... (Add in your own thanksgivings.)

•••••••••••••••• **Intercession** ••••••••••••••••
(Place someone's name in the blank provided.)

Lord, help _____ who is fallen, who is bent beneath his/her load. Lord, lift him/her from this burden.

FROM PSALM 145:14 NIV

•••••••••••••••• **Petition** ••••••••••••••••

Lord, help me meditate on Your majestic, glorious splendor and Your wonderful miracles.

FROM PSALM 145:5 NIV

2

Elohim: God, My Creator

· · · · · · · · · · · · · · · · · · Sally · · · · · · · · · · · · · · · · · ·

*"The LORD God formed man of dust from the
ground, and breathed into his nostrils the breath
of life; and man became a living being."*

GENESIS 2:7

One of our most influential European leaders in Moms in Prayer International, Randi Anita Helvig, was abandoned in South Korea at the age of two. She then lived in an orphanage until she was adopted at age 5. In her new home of Norway, she looked distinctly different than other children. She experienced being bullied and had wounds in her soul from those years, but Jesus healed her heart and gave her freedom.

Both of her parents died while she was in her twenties, and once again it was hard to be alone. She was not sure what God had planned for her, but as she grew in her knowledge of her Creator, she realized He had a great calling for her life. She was not going to waste it.

Today, Randi is a woman filled with God's love, grace, beauty, and a humble strength that comes from knowing who her Creator is. She leads an army of women who pray for the children and schools of Norway and now in other Nordic countries as well. She is an artist and influential leader. Many are following her lead and coming to know who God is and how He created each one of them and their children for a mighty plan and purpose.

I spoke with her college-age daughter who shared with me how her mom's prayers and witness are helping her stand strong when so many students at her college are being pressured to party and to look good on the outside. As she shared with me, it was clear that she understood how God has also created her for an incredible plan and purpose! And she is living out that purpose with freedom and joy. Because both of them know intimately their God who formed them, they are empowered to impact many for Christ and not let anything stand in their way.

Do you know your Creator? Psalm 139:13-17 says, "You formed my inward parts; You wove me in my mother's womb. I will give thanks to You, for I am fearfully and wonderfully made; wonderful are Your works, and my soul knows it very well. My frame was not hidden from You, when I was made in secret, and skillfully wrought in the depths of the earth; Your eyes have seen my unformed substance; and in Your book were all written the days that were ordained for me when yet there was not one of them. How precious also are Your thoughts to me O God! How vast the sum of them."

Do you know this truth? God has created you wonderfully. Before the foundations of the earth He chose you in love to be His own (Ephesians 1:4). You are perfectly crafted with His own hands (Ephesians 2:10). You are imprinted on His hand (Isaiah 49:16). Each day God has ordained for you (Psalm 139:16), before one of them even happens. Every day can be extraordinary when you realize God has created you with His very own hands for an extraordinary life. First Corinthians 2:9 says, "As it is written: 'What no eye has seen, what no ear has heard and what no human mind has conceived: the things God has prepared for those who love him'" (NIV). Ephesians 2:10 says, "We are God's workmanship created in Christ Jesus for good works, which God prepared beforehand so that we would walk in them."

· ·

Every day can be extraordinary when you
realize God has created you with His very
own hands for an extraordinary life.

· ·

When my husband and I worked on the space shuttles as engineers, some designed the shuttle parts and some worked inside the shuttle to prepare it for a gravity-defying mission. But you have the greatest designer of all who created you with a master plan for your life. Not only has God created you for a mighty mission but He will empower you for this purpose.

Ephesians 1:18-21

> I pray that the eyes of your heart may be enlightened, so that you will know what is the hope of His calling, what are the riches of the glory of His inheritance in the saints, and what is the surpassing greatness of His power toward us who believe. These are in accordance with the working of the strength of His might which He brought about in Christ, when He raised Him from the dead and seated Him at His right hand in the heavenly places, far above all rule and authority and power and dominion, and every name that is named, not only in this age but also in the one to come.

The Greek word for power in Ephesians 1:19 is *dunamis* which is dynamic power. The same Creator who spoke the heavens and earth into being and defeated sin is at work within you to accomplish His good work through you.

What is it God wants to do through you? What are you created for? Randi Anita Helvig knows and walks with her Creator "not in persuasive words of wisdom but in demonstration of the Spirit and of power, so that your faith would not rest on the wisdom of men but on the power of God" (1 Corinthians 2:3-5).

God sent forth His disciples clothed in power, and He wants to do the same in your life. But you first need to know Him intimately. Through His Word, the Creator reveals Himself and why He has created you. He will lead you each step of the way if you will be still and know who He is!

Praise

Come let us worship and bow down, let us kneel before the LORD our Maker. For He is our God and we are the people of His pasture and the sheep of His hand.

PSALM 95:6-7

You are my Creator who created me for Your glory and purposes. I cannot conceive what wonders You have in store for me. I praise You that You are working Your glorious purpose within me and throughout creation.

Confession

Since the creation of the world, His invisible attributes, His eternal power and divine nature, have been clearly seen, being understood through what is made, so that they are without excuse. For even though they knew God, they did not honor Him as God or give thanks but they became futile in their speculations and their foolish heart was darkened.

ROMANS 1:20-23

Lord, forgive me for the times I exchange the truth about You for a lie, for worshiping and serving creation instead of You, the Creator.

Thanksgiving

Thank You, Lord, for giving me breath and making me fearfully and wonderfully for Your glory and purpose. I thank You for all of Your creation and how on the seventh day of creation You rested; You had completed what You set out to do. As I step out each day, I know that You ordain my steps for Your glory and purpose.

· · · · · · · · · · · · · · · Intercession · · · · · · · · · · · · · · · ·

Lord, help _____ know You have set him/her apart for Yourself, and You hear _____ when he/she calls to You. Help him/her stop striving and know You are God the Creator. May he/she live life with confidence in You and bring glory to You all of his/her days.

FROM PSALM 4:3 AND PSALM 46:10

· · · · · · · · · · · · · · · Petition · · · · · · · · · · · · · · · · ·

Lord, may I know You have set me apart for Yourself and You hear me when I call to You. May I stop striving and know You are my God my Creator. May I live life with confidence in You and bring glory to You all of my days.

FROM PSALM 4:3 AND PSALM 46:10

3

The Lord Is Worthy of Our Praise

· · · · · · · · · · · · · · · · · · · Cyndie · · · · · · · · · · · · · · · · · · ·

Let all that I am praise the LORD;
with my whole heart, I will praise his holy name.
Let all that I am praise the LORD;
may I never forget the good things he does for me.
He forgives all my sins
and heals all my diseases.
He redeems me from death
and crowns me with love and tender mercies.
He fills my life with good things.
My youth is renewed like the eagle's!

The LORD gives righteousness
and justice to all who are treated unfairly.

He revealed his character to Moses
and his deeds to the people of Israel.
The LORD is compassionate and merciful,
slow to get angry and filled with unfailing love.
He will not constantly accuse us,
nor remain angry forever.
He does not punish us for all our sins;
he does not deal harshly with us, as we deserve.
For his unfailing love toward those who fear him
is as great as the height of the heavens above the earth.
He has removed our sins as far from us
as the east is from the west.

The LORD is like a father to his children,
tender and compassionate to those who fear him.

Praise the LORD, everything he has created,
everything in all his kingdom.

Let all that I am praise the LORD.

PSALM 103:1-13, 22 NLT

*W*e are called to praise the Lord, our Creator and our Savior. Reading just a portion of Psalm 103 gives us ample reason to praise the Lord. He is righteous and compassionate, forgiving and merciful. He heals, and He loves. This beautiful psalm ends with this statement, "Let all that I am praise the LORD." All that we are—our entire being—should praise the Lord. This is not the equivalent of Sunday morning perfunctory singing of a couple church songs. No, this is one's entire being rejoicing about our glorious heavenly Father.

Have you ever been so excited that you actually jumped for joy or squealed with delight? This is the type of praise our heavenly Father deserves... praise that comes from our entire being, standing in awe of the fact that God Almighty loves each one of us individually. And, not only that, He forgives us of our sins so we can be in a love relationship with Him.

When some people think about praying to God, they think of handing Him a laundry list of wants and begging Him to bless those requests with a "yes." But prayer is so much more than that. Prayer is our way to develop a deeper love relationship with our heavenly Father so that when problems come, we can stand unshaken and empowered, keeping our eyes on Him. We can trust Him and know that He loves us and promises to work all things together for good.

In the four steps of prayer, making our requests and interceding in prayer for others creates the very last step. That way we can first spend time developing our relationship with the Lord and preparing our hearts to hear the Holy Spirit's direction when it's time to intercede.

. . . .

Prayer is our way to develop a deeper love
relationship with our heavenly Father so that
when problems come, we can stand unshaken
and empowered, keeping our eyes on Him.

. . . .

We might come to the Lord in prayer because of a problem or stress, but starting with praise reframes our thinking. As soon as we begin praising God, our thoughts are transformed. We're reminded that we're giving this problem over to the God who created the entire universe. Of course, He can take care of whatever concerns us!

. . . . **Praise** . . . .

Lord, I praise You because You are worthy of my praise. You are holy, perfect and righteous, yet You are still loving, compassionate and forgiving. Lord, I do not deserve a relationship with You, yet You mercifully call me into a relationship with You. You want to spend time with me. You want me to share my heart with You, even though You already know my inner thoughts. You beckon me to sit with You, to worship You and Praise You.

. . . . **Confession** . . . .

Lord, forgive me for the times I get so focused on me and my family, I forget to put You first; I forget to praise You. And when I forget to keep my eyes on You, then my problems can seem so overwhelming, because I forget that You are so much bigger than any concern that comes along my path or the path of my child. Forgive me for the times I focus more on the problem instead of You, the Problem Solver. Forgive me for the times that I forget the good things in my life and focus instead on the difficulties.

·············· Thanksgiving ···············

*Lord, I do thank You for the good things in
my life. I specifically thank You for...*

·················· Intercession ·················

*Lord, help _____ remember to praise You, to focus on who
You are, Your power and attributes. As Psalm 103 says in verses 5
and 6, Lord, I pray that You fill _____'s life with good things.
Renew his/her youth like the eagle's. And, Lord, for those who
are being treated unfairly—at school or in our community—
we pray that Your righteousness and justice will prevail.*

·················· Petition ···················

*Oh heavenly Father, may all that I am praise the Lord;
may I never forget the good things You do for me.*

FROM PSALM 103:1-2 NLT

4

Jehovah Jireh: The LORD Provides

· · · · · · · · · · · · · · · · · · · Sally ·

Seeing that His divine power has granted to us everything
pertaining to life and godliness, through the true knowledge
of Him who called us by His own glory and excellence.

2 PETER 1:3

*G*od tells us that those who know the name of God will be strong
and accomplish much for His glory and through His power. It
is important for us as His children to know and understand who our
God is. We need to know Him intimately: by name, by character, by
attribute. He reveals Himself to us through His Word and in our lives.
When we get to know God by name, He will be strong within us and
do great things through us for His glory and great purposes.

One of my favorite names of God is Jehovah Jireh: the LORD Provides. "Jehovah" means the great I AM, the self-existent one! Our Lord
needs nothing from anyone, and yet He has provided everything we
need for life and godliness through His Son. "Jireh" means to see or
foresee. God sees our needs before we do for He is the all-knowing, the
Omniscient God. Matthew 6:8-9 says, "Your Father knows what you
need before you ask Him. Pray, then, in this way: Our Father who is in
heaven, Hallowed be Your name."

In Genesis 22, God reveals Himself to Abraham as the Jehovah
Jireh. Abraham is given a picture of how God would provide salvation
to the world.

> "My father!" And he said, "Here I am, my son." And he
> said, "Behold, the fire and the wood, but where is the
> lamb for the burnt offering?" Abraham said, "God will
> provide for Himself the lamb for the burnt offering, my
> son." So the two of them walked on together...Abraham
> called the name of that place The LORD Will Provide, as
> it is said to this day, "In the mount of the LORD it will be
> provided" (Genesis 22:7-8,14).

As Abraham stood at the altar with his long-awaited son, God provided a ram for a sacrifice. Abraham would not need to give up the son he loved, because God provided a substitute for their sacrifice, just as He did for us. On the same mount Abraham was willing to offer his son Isaac to the Lord, God provided His one and only Son whom He loved as a sacrifice for our sins. Christ's death on the cross and resurrection three days later defeated our enemy and provided the opportunity for us to have a relationship with our Creator and Savior.

As John the Baptist declared during Christ's ministry on earth, "Behold, the Lamb of God who takes away the sin of the world!" (John 1:29).

God continues to provide Himself for our every need. When you have long nights and days of worry and fear about your needs, I pray you will look deeply into God's character and get to know Him as your Jehovah Jireh, as Abraham did.

> He who did not spare His own Son, but delivered Him
> up for us all, how shall He not with Him also freely give
> us all things? (Romans 8:32 NKJV).

Jehovah Jireh has provided a way for us to move from darkness to the light—from being His enemy to being His child.

> You have not received a spirit of slavery leading to fear
> again, but you have received a spirit of adoption as sons
> by which we cry out, "Abba! Father!" (Romans 8:15).

Once we are adopted, God is ready to pour forth provision for this life and the life to come.

If God so clothes the grass of the field, which today is, and tomorrow is thrown into the oven, will He not much more clothe you, O you of little faith? (Matthew 6:30 NKJV).

He doesn't just provide life, but He wants to give us an abundant life! His gift of the Holy Spirit gives power, wisdom, ability to overcome temptation, abundant life, and so much more.

I came that they may have life, and have it abundantly (John 10:10).

If you then, being evil, know how to give good gifts to your children, how much more will your heavenly Father give the Holy Spirit to those who ask Him? (Luke 11:13).

If any of you lacks wisdom, let him ask of God, who gives to all generously and without reproach, and it will be given to him (James 1:5).

Additionally, He has provided for us an eternal home with a new glorious body! We can only imagine how incredible it will be. We will all be walking around perfectly without envy or strife admiring God's finished work!

Ponder this with me: God has provided for our salvation and for all of our needs for life and godliness, our eternal bodies and home. Will He not provide all you need if you but ask?

· · · · · · · · · · · · · · · · · · · Praise · · · · · · · · · · · · · · · · · ·

Lord, I praise You for being my Provider, for meeting my every need, especially my salvation. You know all my needs before I even ask for help, and no need of mine is too small or too great. I can come to You with every request.

Confession

Forgive me, Lord, for being of such little faith! Forgive me for not asking and trusting You. Forgive me for not seeing how You take care of all of Your creation, knowing that You will take much more care of me.

Thanksgiving

Lord, I thank You for providing for all my needs. Today I want to specifically thank You for...

Intercession

Lord, empower _____ to make every effort to add to his/her faith goodness; and to goodness, knowledge; and to knowledge, self-control; and to self-control, perseverance; and to perseverance, godliness; and to godliness, mutual affection; and to mutual affection, love. For if _____ possesses these qualities in increasing measure, they will keep him/her from being ineffective and unproductive in the knowledge of our Lord Jesus Christ.

FROM 2 PETER 1:5-8 NIV

················· **Petition** ·················

*Lord, empower me to make every effort to add to my faith
goodness; and to goodness, knowledge; and to knowledge, self-
control; and to self-control, perseverance; and to perseverance,
godliness; and to godliness, mutual affection; and to mutual
affection, love. For if I possess these qualities in increasing
measure, they will keep me from being ineffective and
unproductive in my knowledge of our Lord Jesus Christ.*

FROM 2 PETER 1:5-8 NIV

5

The Lord Is My Helper

············ Cyndie ············

I lift up my eyes to the mountains—
where does my help come from?
My help comes from the LORD,
the Maker of heaven and earth.

He will not let your foot slip—
he who watches over you will not slumber;
indeed, he who watches over Israel
will neither slumber nor sleep.

The LORD watches over you—
the LORD is your shade at your right hand;
the sun will not harm you by day,
nor the moon by night.

The LORD will keep you from all harm—
he will watch over your life;
the LORD will watch over your coming and going
both now and forevermore.

PSALM 121 NIV

Re-read the passage above, one thought, one sentence at a time. Now take a deep breath. What is the mountain in front of you? What is that rock that might make you stumble? Now imagine the Almighty God, the maker of heaven and earth, peering over that mountain. After all, there is no mountain too big or difficult for Him to conquer. Imagine the Creator of heaven and earth steadying your feet as you begin to climb that mountain. With Him helping you, you know you can conquer not just each step, but each mountain.

Don't you just love the imagery in this Psalm? The one who created every living thing, who placed the moon and the stars in the heavens, who designated every mountain and every rock, not only knows your name, but He loves you. And He comes to your rescue as your helper.

What is the one thing the Psalmist does in this passage? In the very first verse, he says, "I lift up my eyes." Everything else is what God does for us, how He helps us. He will not let your foot slip. He watches over you always, because He never sleeps. He is always on guard, always ready to help. He shades you so neither the sun nor the moon will harm you. He doesn't just help you by protecting you from the sun and the moon. He protects you from all harm and watches over your entire life. No matter where you go, our heavenly Father is there with you, ready to help. We need only to keep our eyes focused on Him. When you are in distress, call out to Him for help, and He will hear you.

Where is your heart today? Do you need to be reminded that God is your help? Or maybe He is calling you to pray for someone else, that they will remember God is their help and to call out to Him.

We think of King David as a mighty warrior, a forgiven man with a heart after God. Often we forget that David was hunted down by King Saul, who wanted to destroy him. David had seen God rescue him before and knew his Savior would help him.

Psalm 18:4-6; 32-36 NIV

The cords of death entangled me;
the torrents of destruction overwhelmed me.
The cords of the grave coiled around me;
the snares of death confronted me.
In my distress I called to the Lord;
I cried to my God for help.
From his temple he heard my voice;
my cry came before him, into his ears. ...

It is God who arms me with strength
and keeps my way secure.
He makes my feet like the feet of a deer;
he causes me to stand on the heights.
He trains my hands for battle;
my arms can bend a bow of bronze.
You make your saving help my shield,
and your right hand sustains me;
your help has made me great.
You provide a broad path for my feet,
so that my ankles do not give way.

In verse 35, David acknowledges that God's "saving help" has been his sustaining shield. He summarizes, "your help has made me great."

....

Where is your heart today? Do you need
to be reminded that God is your help?

....

And, just like Psalm 121, this passage describes how God helps us. He helps by strengthening us, keeping us secure and sure-footed even on the difficult mountains of life. In verses 33 and 36, he uses again the analogy of climbing over treacherous terrain.

God doesn't lift us off the character-shaping mountains in our lives. He offers His help, strength, and power for us to endure it. Instead of allowing us to stumble and fall, He empowers us, making us sure-footed like the deer (verse 33) and providing a broad path for us to walk on safely and without injury. Our heavenly Father doesn't pluck us out of the ordeal. He guides and protects us as we learn and grow every step of the way. In fact, it's when we need His help that we are at our strongest, because we allow Him to work through us.

As Paul says in 2 Corinthians 12:9-10, "He said to me, 'My grace is sufficient for you, for my power is made perfect in weakness.' Therefore I will boast all the more gladly about my weaknesses, so that Christ's power may rest on me. That is why, for Christ's sake, I delight in weaknesses, in insults, in hardships, in persecutions, in difficulties. For when I am weak, then I am strong" (NIV).

· · · · · · · · · · · · · · · · · Praise · · · · · · · · · · · · · · · · ·

Oh, Lord, we praise You for providing help when we feel overwhelmed, unsure, and shaky. When we call on Your holy name, You straighten the path, secure our steps, give us the "mind of Christ," and empower us through our weaknesses. You help us look past the mountains in front of us and gaze at the one who created every mountain, every star, every rock. Lord, I praise You that You use the obstacles to strengthen me and my character. How amazing it is that the heavenly Father and Creator cares about me. Thank You!

· · · · · · · · · · · · · · · · Confession · · · · · · · · · · · · · · · ·

Lord, please forgive me for the times that my eyes slip off of You and onto every obstacle in front of me, the big and the little. Help me, Lord, to remember to focus my eyes on You.

· · · · · · · · · · · · · · · Thanksgiving · · · · · · · · · · · · · · ·

As I think back on all the times You have helped me, Lord, I want to say thank You specifically for helping me through this situation...

· · · · · · · · · · · · · · · · Intercession · · · · · · · · · · · · · · · ·

*Lord, I pray that _____ will call on You for help, that he/she
will stop looking at the mountain, but will look, instead
at You. Where does _____'s help come from? It's not from
me, but from You, the maker of heaven and earth. Lord, please
do not let _____'s foot slip. Shade him/her from harm,
especially from the harmful glare of the evil one. Watch over
_____'s comings and goings, both now and forevermore.*

FROM PSALM 121

· · · · · · · · · · · · · · · · Petition · · · · · · · · · · · · · · · ·

*Lord, no matter what comes my way, remind me that my
help comes from You, the Maker of heaven and earth.*

FROM PSALM 121:2

6

Jehovah Sabaoth: The Lord of Hosts

· · · · · · · · · · · · · · · · · · · Sally · · · · · · · · · · · · · · · · · · ·

*Who is this King of glory? The Lord of
hosts, He is the King of glory. Selah.*

PSALM 24:10

*a*re you weary, tired, and feel like the whole world is against you?
Do you feel like you have no strength to fight? Does the evening
news make you anguish and want to give up? If you were sitting across
my kitchen counter I would tell you to run to Jehovah Sabaoth, the
Lord of hosts!

Psalm 46:6-8

The nations made an uproar, the kingdoms tottered; He
raised His voice, the earth melted. The Lord of hosts
is with us; the God of Jacob is our stronghold. Selah.
Come, behold the works of the Lord.

Jehovah Sabaoth will strengthen you, fight victoriously for you, and
He will give you rest and peace. Proverbs 18:10 says, "The name of the
Lord is a strong tower; the righteous runs into it and is safe."

In the Old Testament, when Hannah was provoked by her "rival,"
where did she go? She ran to Jehovah Sabaoth, the Lord of hosts!

Her rival, however, would provoke her bitterly to irri-
tate her, because the Lord had closed her womb. It

41

happened year after year, as often as she went up to the house of the LORD, she would provoke her; so she wept and would not eat. Then Elkanah her husband said to her, "Hannah, why do you weep and why do you not eat and why is your heart sad? Am I not better to you than ten sons?"

Then Hannah rose after eating and drinking in Shiloh. Now Eli the priest was sitting on the seat by the doorpost of the temple of the LORD. She, greatly distressed, prayed to the LORD and wept bitterly. She made a vow and said, "O LORD of hosts, if You will indeed look on the affliction of Your maidservant and remember me, and not forget Your maidservant, but will give Your maidservant a son, then I will give him to the LORD all the days of his life, and a razor shall never come on his head" (1 Samuel 1:6-11).

This was the cry of the heart of a woman who was teased mercilessly because, in a culture where a woman's worth was wrapped up in her children, she could not conceive. Hannah called on Jehovah Sabaoth because she needed victory over her situation. While God does not always answer our prayers exactly as we request, He did for Hannah, and she gave birth to Samuel, one of the great prophets in the Old Testament.

It does not matter the size of our enemy, Jehovah Sabaoth is still the answer. After growing into a man of God, Hannah's son Samuel anointed a young shepherd named David to eventually become king of Israel. While David was still in his youth, he willingly faced a giant!

The Philistine [Goliath the giant] also said to David, "Come to me, and I will give your flesh to the birds of the sky and the beasts of the field." Then David said to the Philistine, "You come to me with a sword, a spear, and a javelin, but I come to you in the name of the LORD

of hosts, the God of the armies of Israel, whom you have
taunted. This day the LORD will deliver you up into my
hands" (1 Samuel 17:44-46).

Are you facing a giant of a problem today? Call upon the LORD
Sabaoth, and He will fight for you.

I witness women all over the world facing seemingly insurmount-
able situations: military tanks rolling into their towns, ISIS taking their
lands, diseases like AIDS wiping out a generation in their villages, ter-
minal cancer destroying their bodies, children immersed in addiction.
I watch as they call on Jehovah Sabaoth and they become empowered
to walk courageously and victoriously. "This is the word of the Lord
to Zerubbabel saying, 'Not by might nor by power, but by My Spirit,'
says the LORD of hosts" (Zechariah 4:6).

In the Old Testament battle of Jericho, God worked through His
people to bring down the walls of Jericho, making their enemies' hearts
melt with fear, and giving the Israelites the victory. Before that was possible, Joshua met the Captain of the LORD's host: Jesus incarnate!

> It came about when Joshua was by Jericho, that he lifted
> up his eyes and looked, and behold, a man was stand-
> ing opposite him with his sword drawn in his hand, and
> Joshua went to him and said to him, "Are you for us or
> for our adversaries?" He said, "No; rather I indeed come
> now *as* captain of the host of the LORD." And Joshua fell
> on his face to the earth, and bowed down, and said to
> him, "What has my lord to say to his servant?" The cap-
> tain of the LORD's host said to Joshua, "Remove your
> sandals from your feet, for the place where you are stand-
> ing is holy." And Joshua did so (Joshua 5:13-15).

What walls do you need to bring down? Maybe there are walls in
your family or in your marriage? Has your heart become hard against
others or against God? Allow Jehovah Sabaoth to bring down the walls
as you worship Him. What land do you need the LORD of hosts to fight
for? Is it your home, neighborhood, or country?

May you be like Hannah, David, Joshua, and the others who fell on their faces, worshipping Jehovah Sabaoth and crying out to the LORD of hosts for help.

· · · · · · · · · · · · · · · · · · **Praise** · · · · · · · · · · · · · · · · · ·

Lord, I praise You for commanding the heavenly hosts and fighting for me, for bringing victory to Your people.

There is none like the God of Jeshurun, who rides the heavens to your help, and through the skies in His majesty. The eternal is a dwelling place, and underneath are the everlasting arms; and He drove out the enemy from before you, and said, "Destroy!"

DEUTERONOMY 33:26-27

· · · · · · · · · · · · · · · · · · **Confession** · · · · · · · · · · · · · · · · · ·

Lord, search my heart and consider my ways. Test me, so that I may be clean and righteous before You.

· · · · · · · · · · · · · · · · · · **Thanksgiving** · · · · · · · · · · · · · · · · · ·

Thank You that the battle is not mine. It is You who fights for me! "Thanks be to God, who gives us the victory through our Lord Jesus Christ" (1 Corinthians 15:57).

· · · · · · · · · · · · · · · · · · **Intercession** · · · · · · · · · · · · · · · · · ·

Lord, answer _____ in the day of trouble! May the name of the God of Jacob set _____ securely on high! Send him/her help and support. Grant _____ the desires of his/her heart.

FROM PSALM 20:1-4

· · · · · · · · · · · · · · · · · · · **Petition** · · · · · · · · · · · · · · · · · ·

I trust that You will answer me in the day of trouble. May the name of the God of Jacob set me securely on high and send help and support. Lord, please grant me the desires of my heart.

FROM PSALM 20:1-4

7

God Is Love

Cyndie

The LORD your God is living among you.
He is a mighty savior.
He will take delight in you with gladness.
With his love, he will calm all your fears.
He will rejoice over you with joyful songs.

ZEPHANIAH 3:17 NLT

hen I was in college, I discovered the verse Zephaniah 3:17 tucked into a small card pack of encouraging Bible verses. Even though I had accepted Christ as my personal savior when I was a wee little four-year-old, my young-adult mind could not grasp what I was reading. God actually *delights* in me? With *gladness*? He *rejoices over me with joyful songs*? That could not be right, I thought. The cards must have a misprint!

Sure, I knew John 3:16, "This is how God loved the world: He gave his one and only Son, so that everyone who believes in him will not perish but have eternal life" (NLT). That amazing love is filled with God's grace, mercy, and sacrifice. But, did the Holy God really delight in me?

In my disbelief, I determined to look up the verse. And there it was in black and white in my personal Bible. My brain could barely comprehend this. The God who created the universe might actually delight in me and love me so much that He rejoices over me with singing and calms me with His love? Astounding!

As an adolescent, I could never quite grasp God's love. People talked about it all the time, but I couldn't understand that the One who designed the whole world could really love me, personally. He knew me even better than I did, and, well, I could be rather annoying. I assumed He tolerated me, at best. I had a misguided sense that God loved humanity collectively, but that he'd rather strike us dead for all of our naughtiness or, in biblical terms, "unrighteousness." The funny thing is, I was a pretty good kid. But growing up in a fairly legalistic church, I focused more on the dos and don'ts than on the fact that God loved me unconditionally, no matter what.

But let me say it again: He truly does delight in me—and in you!

When I gave birth to my own children, I finally understood this kind of love. When my toddlers smiled, giggled, or learned something new, I delighted in them with gladness. And, yes, there were many times my love and delight for them boiled up inside me, and I burst out in song, or, as Zephaniah 3:17 says, "rejoice over you with joyful songs" (NLT). And, like most parents, I frequently had the opportunity to calm my children's fears with my love.

When my daughter was little, new circumstances often made her fearful. But safe in my arms, she would watch swimming lessons or gymnastics or kids playing at a park, until her anxiety subsided and she felt courageous enough to venture out. My love calmed her fears. Likewise, God's love can calm our fears. Yet the mystery of His love is that we never have to leave the safety and comfort of His protective arms. We don't have to venture out on our own. His love carries us through, and He empowers us to weather any storm.

Once we realize that God loves us completely, we can trust that He will indeed work all things together for good (Romans 8:28). As Psalm 52:8 so beautifully explains, "I am like an olive tree flourishing in the house of God; I trust in God's unfailing love for ever and ever" (NIV).

As I meditate on the idea of a love that delights, I can't help but think of a faithful church volunteer and her husband. Each time I see them together, they are holding hands and smiling as if they were newlyweds. Mind you, this couple is in their eighties! One day I asked how long they had been married. "Forty-five years," Jodie said with a smile. "He was the answer to my son's prayers." Yep, that caught my attention, too! "Your *son's* prayers?" I asked. "Yes, he was about 15 at the time, and he prayed that he could finally have a good dad." She then explained that her first husband was "cruel," an abusive alcoholic that had so wounded her oldest son, that he began saving up money to change his name legally so he would no longer be associated with his biological father. Then along came the answer to her son's prayer: a handsome, kind dentist who not only swept this single mother off her feet, but delighted the children and extended family, as well. His love for her and her children was unmistakable. With tears in her eyes, Jodie shared how, even though her oldest son was just about an adult when she re-married, her new husband legally adopted him so he would know that he would always be loved and cared for and delighted in— and so he could be grafted into a new family legacy. Even though her son is now in his sixties, Jodie always knows when he calls, because her husband answers with sheer love and delight, "Ah, my son!"

· ·

Once we realize that God loves us completely,
we can trust that He will indeed work all
things together for good (Romans 8:28).

· ·

What a beautiful picture of God loving us and delighting in us so much that He rejoices over adopting us into His heavenly family.

· · · · · · · · · · · · · · · · · **Praise** · · · · · · · · · · · · · · · · · · ·

Lord, I praise You for loving us unconditionally. You are a mighty
Savior, who delights in me with gladness. With Your love, You
can calm all my fears. You rejoice over me with joyful songs.

From Zephaniah 3:17

Confession

Lord, please forgive me for the times I forget how much You love me and delight in me.

Thanksgiving

Lord, thank You for loving me so much that You died on the cross for my sins, and that I can be part of Your family. Thank You that Your love can calm my fears, because it reminds me that I can trust You.

Intercession

Lord, out of Your glorious riches, strengthen _____ with Your power through Your Spirit in his/her inner being, so that Christ may dwell in his/her heart through faith. And I pray that _____, being rooted and established in love, may have power, together with all the Lord's holy people, to grasp how wide and long and high and deep the love of Christ is, and to know this love that surpasses knowledge — that he/she may be filled to the measure of all the fullness of You.

From Ephesians 3:16-19

Petition

Lord, out of Your glorious riches, strengthen me with Your power through Your Spirit in my inner being, so that Christ may dwell in my heart through faith. And I pray that I will be rooted and established in love, so that I may have power, together with all the Lord's holy people, to grasp how wide and long and high and deep is the love of Christ, and to know this love that surpasses knowledge — that I may be filled to the measure of all the fullness of You.

From Ephesians 3:16-19

8

God Our Hope

· · · · · · · · · · · · · · · · · · · Sally · · · · · · · · · · · · · · · · · · ·

May the God of hope fill you with all joy and
peace in believing, so that you will abound
in hope by the power of the Holy Spirit.

ROMANS 15:13

beautiful, tall, regal woman dressed in her exquisite African clothes representing her nation came into my office one day. She had scars on her face, yet held herself with great poise and purpose. She wanted to tell me what God was doing in her country through Moms in Prayer International. But first she shared with me her story. Her father did not want her mother or her, so they were sent away. At a young age she learned to dig for food and carry water. One day there was a fire, and they lost everything and had to begin again. This loss left scars on her body and heart.

When she was 14, she was planning to end her life. She was planning to set another fire to their home so she and her mom would not have to struggle to survive. She went down to get water that very day and the God of Hope met her there. She explained to me that Jesus spoke to her heart, and she realized He alone was her hope. Her life turned around; God provided what she needed for school, and even though she was far behind the other children, God gave her hope to continue on.

Her trust in Him was not wasted. She lived out Romans 5:5: "Hope does not disappoint, because the love of God has been poured out within our hearts through the Holy Spirit who was given to us." God gave her the ability to become a great translator! She was astonished and so were others around her. This gift allowed her to translate for women from Moms in Prayer who share God's hope through prayer to villagers, as they teach women who God is and how to pray. She translates for missionaries of other organizations too. She is using her God-given gift to bring her nation the hope that saved her and her family. As a mother of several children, she prays for them, knowing her hope is in God. She has hope here on earth and for an eternal future.

The biblical definition of hope is a favorable and confident expectation; the happy expectation of good! As you learn to place your hope in God, you will have a confident expectation in your heart and know that Christ in you is the hope of glory (Colossians 1:27) and your hope is eternal (Titus 3:7).

Do you have hope today? God wants us to know the great hope of our calling! He tells us in Ephesians 1:18-19, "That you will know what is the hope of His calling, what are the riches of the glory of His inheritance in the saints, and what is the surpassing greatness of His power toward us who believe. These are in accordance with the working of the strength of His might."

As I am writing this chapter, I am meeting with women from 19 different countries. They are gathering together to call out to the God of hope for this next generation! He is giving them great expectations of what He will do as they pray! "I hope in You O LORD; You will answer, O Lord my God" (Psalm 38:15).

One mom has shared how her son rebelled against God and his family. She hurt badly for him and her family, but she never gave up hope in God. "By two unchangeable things in which it is impossible for God to lie, we who have taken refuge would have strong encouragement to take hold of the hope set before us. This hope we have as an anchor of the soul, a hope both sure and steadfast..." (Hebrews 6:18-19). Her son moved to South Africa thinking he was going there for surfing and work. It was there he found his way to back to God and his family and met a Christian wife.

Another woman has shared with me how she fears she has permanently damaged her marriage and her children, who are now adults. As her family struggled with finances, the way she spoke to and about her husband were very cruel. During our time together, as she repented from her attitude and actions, my prayer for her was: "May our Lord Jesus Christ Himself and God our Father, who has loved us and given us eternal comfort and good hope by grace, comfort and strengthen your hearts in every good work and word" (2 Thessalonians 2:16-17).

Have you lost all hope? Don't look at others, this world, or yourself for help. Look up and know the God of hope. "Why are you in despair, O my soul? And why have you become disturbed within me? Hope in God, for I shall yet praise Him, the help of my countenance and my God" (Psalm 42:11).

. . . .

There is always hope when we include God.

. . . .

God is our hope. Open up His Word and drink deeply of the hope waiting to be revealed. May your eyes be open and may this truth go deep within your soul. "Whatever was written in earlier times was written for our instruction, so that through perseverance and the encouragement of the Scriptures we might have hope" (Romans 15:4).

. . . . **Praise** . . . .

Remember my affliction and my wandering, the wormwood and bitterness. Surely my soul remembers and is bowed down within me. This I recall to my mind, therefore I have hope. The LORD's lovingkindnesses indeed never cease, for His compassions never fail. They are new every morning; great is Your faithfulness. "The LORD is my portion," says my soul, "Therefore I have hope in Him." The LORD is good to those who wait for Him, to the person who seeks Him. It is good that he waits silently for the salvation of the LORD.

LAMENTATIONS 3:19-26

Confession

Lord, forgive me when I look everywhere else for hope! Forgive me when I do not look to You with great expectations of what You will do in my life and situations. Forgive me when I have lost my trust in You!

Thanksgiving

Lord, thank You that as I hope in You, You will answer, O Lord my God.

FROM PSALM 38:15

Thank You for this answer to prayer...

Intercession

I pray that the God of our Lord Jesus Christ, the Father of glory, may give to _____ a spirit of wisdom and of revelation in the knowledge of You. I pray that the eyes of _____'s heart may be enlightened, so that he/she will know what is the hope of Your calling, what are the riches of the glory of Your inheritance in the saints, and what is the surpassing greatness of Your power toward us who believe, in accordance with the working of the strength of Your might.

FROM EPHESIANS 1:17-19

· · · · · · · · · · · · · · · · · · · **Petition** ·

I pray that the God of our Lord Jesus Christ, the Father of glory,
will give me a spirit of wisdom and of revelation in the knowledge
of You. I pray that the eyes of my heart will be enlightened, so
that I will know what is the hope of Your calling, what are the
riches of the glory of Your inheritance in the saints, and what
is the surpassing greatness of Your power toward us who believe,
in accordance with the working of the strength of Your might.

FROM EPHESIANS 1:17-19

9

God Overflows with Mercy

· · · · · · · · · · · · · · · · · Cyndie · · · · · · · · · · · · · · · · ·

Praise be to the God and Father of our Lord Jesus Christ!
In his great mercy he has given us new birth into a living
hope through the resurrection of Jesus Christ from the
dead, and into an inheritance that can never perish, spoil
or fade. This inheritance is kept in heaven for you.

1 PETER 1:3-4 NIV

O h how we praise the Lord for His great mercy! How amazing that
our heavenly Father, who is perfect and holy, has such great mercy
on each of us individually, that He forgives us of our sins and desires to
have a relationship with us.

Ask Siri for a definition of Mercy, and a sweet voice will define
it as "compassion or forgiveness shown toward someone whom it is
within one's power to punish or harm." Google adds to the definition:
"An event to be grateful for, especially because its occurrence prevents
something unpleasant or provides relief from suffering."

The Creator of the entire universe chose to grant you and me mercy
by showing compassion and forgiveness instead of banishing us from
His presence because of our sin. And what is the "something unpleasant" that we no longer need to suffer from? That's the intense agony of
being separated from God for all of eternity. Yet, out of His great mercy,
He forgave us and invited us into His family.

Think about your worst sin: something you really regret. God
chooses to forgive even that. Yes, THAT sin. Because of His great

mercy, found through the sacrifice of Jesus Christ for our sins, we can have a relationship with the holy, perfect God. That mercy is what sets Christianity apart from other religions that maintain lists of dos and don'ts—what to eat, what not to eat, how to wash one's hands, how often to pray, when to pray, etc.

There is only one way to become a Christian and that is to humbly repent of our sins and to freely accept Christ as our Lord and Savior. Everything else we might do or not do is out of our love relationship with the Lord. There is nothing else required to begin that relationship, to be considered a Christian. The entire payment for our sins was completed by Jesus Christ. This free gift was, as one might say, "signed, sealed, and delivered." All we have to do is accept it. Now that is mercy!

Take a moment to meditate on Titus 3:4-6, "When the kindness and love of God our Savior appeared, he saved us, not because of righteous things we had done, but because of his mercy. He saved us through the washing of rebirth and renewal by the Holy Spirit, whom he poured out on us generously through Jesus Christ our Savior" (NIV).

We can have a relationship with Christ, not because of anything we have done, but "because of his mercy." Wow. Take a moment to really praise the Lord for loving you so much that He showers you with His mercy so you can enjoy a relationship with Him.

Yet, God's amazing mercy doesn't stop at salvation. James 5:11 says, "The Lord is full of compassion and mercy" (NIV). And Hebrews 4:15-16 describes it so beautifully here: "We do not have a high priest who is unable to empathize with our weaknesses, but we have one who has been tempted in every way, just as we are—yet he did not sin. Let us then approach God's throne of grace with confidence, so that we may receive mercy and find grace to help us in our time of need" (NIV).

How is your relationship with the Lord? Do you find it hard to sit still before Him because of unconfessed sin in your life? Sometimes, when we forget God's great mercy and compassion and forgiveness and grace, we avoid spending time with Him. We skip out on church or Bible study, and skirt around all spiritual conversations. But God knows our hearts. He knows our deepest thoughts. Trust His great mercy and compassion, and be honest with Him. Admitting our fears and anger and frustration to our heavenly Father allows us to be washed anew in His great mercy, where we find healing and peace.

I love the complete honesty found in the Psalms. Psalm 30:8-12 exemplifies being honest with God (albeit with a bit of sass) and the result, "You turned my wailing into dancing...I will praise you forever" (NIV).

> To you, LORD, I called;
> to the LORD I cried for mercy:
> "What is gained if I am silenced,
> if I go down to the pit?
> Will the dust praise you?
> Will it proclaim your faithfulness?
> Hear, LORD, and be merciful to me;
> LORD, be my help."

> You turned my wailing into dancing;
> you removed my sackcloth and clothed me with joy,
> that my heart may sing your praises and not be silent.
> LORD my God, I will praise you forever
> (Psalm 30:8-12 NIV).

· · · · · · · · · · · · · · · · · · · Praise · · · · · · · · · · · · · · · · · · ·

Lord, I praise You for Your saving mercy. I pray today with the words of David: "Praise be to the LORD, for he has heard my cry for mercy. The LORD is my strength and my shield; my heart trusts in him, and he helps me. My heart leaps for joy, and with my song I praise him. The LORD is the strength of his people, a fortress of salvation for his anointed one" (Psalm 28:6-8 NIV).

· · · · · · · · · · · · · · · · · Confession · · · · · · · · · · · · · · · · ·

Lord, forgive me for the times I forget about Your mercy and compassion and try to hide my sins and emotions from You. Specifically, I confess to You the sin of _____.

· · · · · · · · · · · · · · · · Thanksgiving · · · · · · · · · · · · · · ·

Lord, I so thank You for forgiving me of my sins, for showing me mercy when I did not deserve it. Thank You, Almighty Father.

· · · · · · · · · · · · · · · · · Intercession · · · · · · · · · · · · · · · ·

Lord, I pray for _____, who does not yet know You. In Your great mercy, grant _____ new birth into a living hope through the resurrection of Jesus Christ from the dead, and into an inheritance that can never perish, spoil, or fade.

FROM 1 PETER 1:3-4

· · · · · · · · · · · · · · · · · Petition · · · · · · · · · · · · · · · · · ·

Hear, Lord, and be merciful to me; Lord, be my help. Turn my wailing into dancing, and clothe me with Your joy, that my heart may sing Your praises and not be silent. Lord my God, I will praise You forever.

FROM PSALM 30:10-12 NIV

10

Run to Adonai

I know that the LORD is great
And that our Lord is above all gods.

PSALM 135:5

I had spent my life running after my own dreams and goals, but one day I met God heart-to-heart. As I was reading my Bible and realized that Jesus was God, I knew I had to bow my knee and confess Him as Lord. Philippians 2:8-11 says, "Being found in appearance as a man, He humbled Himself by becoming obedient to the point of death, even death on a cross. For this reason also, God highly exalted Him, and bestowed on Him the name which is above every name, so that at the name of Jesus EVERY KNEE WILL BOW, of those who are in heaven and on earth and under the earth, and that every tongue will confess that Jesus Christ is Lord, to the glory of God the Father."

You see, sooner or later everyone will recognize Jesus as Lord. Sooner is better than later. After we receive Jesus as our Lord, this becomes His role in our lives each day, if we allow this.

Dr. James Dobson was one of my mentors as a young mom, and I would listen to his radio broadcast each day. Recently, when I was on his radio show he asked me if I missed the excitement of working on the Space Shuttle and witnessing what it could do. I shared with Dr. Dobson how my life is filled with greater excitement because I have made Jesus my Lord. I am on the most amazing journey one could imagine. I am on God's team to build His kingdom.

Keep your eyes on *Jesus*, who both began and finished this race we're in. Study how he did it. Because he never lost sight of where he was headed—that exhilarating finish in and with God—he could put up with anything along the way: Cross, shame, whatever. And now he's *there*, in the place of honor, right alongside God. When you find yourselves flagging in your faith, go over that story again, item by item, that long litany of hostility he plowed through. *That* will shoot adrenaline into your souls! (Hebrews 12:2-3 MSG).

Have you ever watched a shepherd and his sheep dog work together to take care of their sheep? The sheep dog waits intently at the feet of his shepherd, who sends the sheep dog forth to help the sheep to greener pastures or by still water or toward rest.

·····························

After we receive Jesus as our Lord, this becomes
His role in our lives each day, if we allow this.

·····························

The first time in Scripture that we see the name Adonai is in Genesis 15:2, "Abram said, 'O Lord GOD, what will You give me, since I am childless, and the heir of my house is Eliezer of Damascus?'" The word Lord means master, supreme in authority, controller, absolute ruler. Abram was familiar with being a master. He had many servants under him. He took care of their every need. And they served alongside him to fulfill the great calling God had for this man who was about to become a nation.

Our Lord and master is the King of kings, Lord of lords, the Great I Am, almighty, all-powerful, all-knowing, sovereign, perfect, majestic God. He lives to intercede for us and so much more. You have a great calling on your life, so you must get your heart, mind, and soul in such a place that you have no will of your own, only the will of the Father. If you do this, He will lead you on the greatest journey you could ever imagine. Each day I surrender my heart and acknowledge Him as Lord, I can hear His voice leading my way. He never disappoints me.

Matthew 6:9-10 says, "Pray, then, in this way: 'Our Father who is in heaven, hallowed be Your name. Your kingdom come. Your will be done, on earth as it is in heaven.'" Jesus lives within us and can accomplish God's will here on earth through us! That is His heart's desire! "For it is God who works in you to will and to act in order to fulfill his good purpose" (Philippians 2:13 NIV).

Jesus demonstrated to us when He surrendered His will to God that He was empowered to accomplish God's great will. When we acknowledge Jesus as Lord, He will empower us to fulfill His great will. Do you acknowledge Him as Lord over all in your life?

Ephesians 1:19-23

What is the surpassing greatness of His power toward us who believe. These are in accordance with the working of the strength of His might which He brought about in Christ, when He raised Him from the dead and seated Him at His right hand in the heavenly places, far above all rule and authority and power and dominion, and every name that is named, not only in this age but also in the one to come. And He put all things in subjection under His feet, and gave Him as head over all things to the church, which is His body, the fullness of Him who fills all in all.

In Luke 22:42-43 Jesus prayed in Gethsemane, "'Father, if You are willing, remove this cup from Me; yet not My will, but Yours be done.' Now an angel from heaven appeared to Him, strengthening Him." God empowered Him to face His enemies and face the cross! He defeated all our enemies through the cross. And now, "what is the surpassing greatness of His power toward us who believe. These are in accordance with the working of the strength of His might which He brought about in Christ, when He raised Him from the dead and seated Him at His right hand in the heavenly *places*, far above all rule and authority and power and dominion, and every name that is named, not only in this age but also in the one to come. And He put all things in subjection under His feet, and gave Him as head over all things to the church, which is His body, the fullness of Him who fills all in all."

Don't miss out on what He has for you. Heed His warnings:

> Why do you call Me, "Lord, Lord," and do not do what I say? (Luke 6:46).

> Not everyone who says to Me, "Lord, Lord," will enter the kingdom of heaven, but he who does the will of My Father who is in heaven will enter (Matthew 7:21).

> Many plans are in a man's heart, but the counsel of the LORD will stand (Proverbs 19:21).

As you begin each day, surrender it to the Lord and He will empower you to fulfill His mighty call on your life. If you have never surrendered to Jesus as Savior, may today be the day of your salvation.

Romans 10:8-10

> What does it say? "The word is near you, in your mouth and in your heart"—that is, the word of faith which we are preaching, that if you confess with your mouth Jesus as Lord, and believe in your heart that God raised Him from the dead, you will be saved; for with the heart a person believes, resulting in righteousness, and with the mouth he confesses, resulting in salvation.

· · · · · · · · · · · · · · · · · · **Praise** · · · · · · · · · · · · · · · · · ·

O LORD, our LORD, How majestic is Your name in all the earth, who have displayed Your splendor above the heavens!

PSALM 8:1

*You are Lord over all and You do as You please among the
inhabitants of Your people. I acknowledge You as Lord of my life.*

Confession

*Lord forgive me when I call You Lord, but do not
do what You tell me. I ask forgiveness for...*

Thanksgiving

*Give thanks to the Lord of lords,
For His lovingkindness is everlasting.*

PSALM 136:3

I specifically thank You for...

Intercession

*I pray that_____ may be filled with the knowledge of Your
will in all spiritual wisdom and understanding, so that he/she
will walk in a manner worthy of You, to please You in all respects,
bearing fruit in every good work and increasing in the knowledge
of You; strengthened with all power, according to Your glorious
might, for the attaining of all steadfastness and patience; joyously.*

FROM COLOSSIANS 1:9-11

· · · · · · · · · · · · · · · · · · · **Petition** · · · · · · · · · · · · · · · · · · ·

Lord, help me be filled with the knowledge of Your will in all
spiritual wisdom and understanding, so that I will walk in
a manner worthy of You, to please You in all respects, bearing
fruit in every good work and increasing in the knowledge of You;
strengthened with all power, according to Your glorious might,
for the attaining of all steadfastness and patience; joyously.

FROM COLOSSIANS 1:9-11

Empowered Through Confession

efore we come before the pure and holy God, we must acknowledge our sins and repent of them. This restores our relationship with Him and allows us to more effectively hear the Holy Spirit as we lift up our requests to Him through intercession and petition. Want to be empowered through Christ? We must first cleanse our imperfect vessels through confession, so we can be a clean vessel in which the Holy Spirit can indwell and empower.

> *If I had not confessed the sin in my heart,*
> *the Lord would not have listened.*

PSALM 66:18 NLT

11

The Cure for the Spiritual Blahs

· · · · · · · · · · · · · · · · Cyndie · · · · · · · · · · · · · · · ·

Come and listen, all you who fear God,
and I will tell you what he did for me.
For I cried out to him for help,
praising him as I spoke.
If I had not confessed the sin in my heart,
the Lord would not have listened. But God did listen!
He paid attention to my prayer.
Praise God, who did not ignore my prayer
or withdraw his unfailing love from me.

PSALM 66:16-20 NLT

o you ever feel like God has withdrawn His love from you? Do you wonder what happened to the warm fuzzy feeling when you first stepped out in faith for Christ? Do you sometimes sit down to pray, yet feel a disconnection with the heavenly Father?

Often, the spiritual "blahs" can mean that you have unconfessed sin in your life. Is there a sin that God keeps tapping at your heart to confess, but you enjoy holding onto it? Take anger, for example. We don't like to admit it, but sometimes we enjoy holding onto anger, don't we? We ponder what led to our anger. Then we stew over it, complaining to our friends and loved ones. Sometimes anger can be invigorating, so we grab onto it as tightly as a puppy clenches onto a chew toy. We don't want to let go of it.

Other situations and emotions can separate us from intimacy with our Creator. If you've had recent conflict with another person, you might be regretting the words you yelled at them, while defensively rationalizing that the person deserved such comments. Or maybe you are creating the distance between you and God as you avoid church, your quiet time, or Christian friends, because you know God might convict you. And, well, you don't want to be convicted, because, you assert that you're quite content with your decisions.

The downside, however, is that without confession and getting right with the Lord, you can't become a clean vessel before Him, so that He can fully empower you to live the life He planned for you. Imagine using a hole-filled colander as a flower vase. What would happen? You'd keep filling the vase, but it would be leaking water. Not only would it be messy, but the flowers would soon shrivel up and die. Instead of a beautiful arrangement with an exquisite aroma, you'd have a bouquet of decay with the horrible stench of mold.

2 Corinthians 4:2,7 NIV

> We have renounced secret and shameful ways; we do not use deception, nor do we distort the word of God. On the contrary, by setting forth the truth plainly we commend ourselves to everyone's conscience in the sight of God... But we have this treasure in jars of clay to show that this all-surpassing power is from God and not from us.

God lovingly handcrafted each one of us for a specific purpose. When we confess our sins and create a clear channel between ourselves and our Lord, then God fills us with His power to accomplish His will. Do you want to not only stand firm through trials but to also fulfill God's purpose for your life? You must confess your sins to the Lord to prepare yourself to be an empty vessel that can be filled with the Holy Spirit.

Do you want your prayers answered? Then you need to be able to stand in the name of Christ Jesus, holy before the heavenly Father. If you have asked Christ into your heart, asking forgiveness of your sins and professing faith in the Savior, you are part of the family of God. No one can snatch you out of the Father's hand (John 10:29). Yet, we must daily—and often many times a day—ask forgiveness of our sins, so the Lord can forgive us, and make us whole (not holey, like the colander).

. . . .

When we confess our sins and create a clear
channel between ourselves and our Lord, then
God fills us with His power to accomplish His will.

. . . .

I love that Psalm 66 lists all the elements of the four steps of prayer: praising God for who He is, thanking God for what He's done, confessing sins, and crying out for help. But the key is in verse 18, "If I had not confessed the sin in my heart, the Lord would not have listened" (NLT).

Do you want the Lord to hear your prayers? Make sure you are clean before Him. Take some time right now. Is there a sin that you're holding onto? Is there something you need to confess to the Lord? Look at verse 20, "Praise God, who did not ignore my prayer or withdraw his unfailing love from me " (NLT). The Lord's love is unfailing, meaning, you can't do anything that will cause His love to fail. So what do you have to lose?

As you pray through the four steps below, ask, as David did in Psalm 139:23-24, "Search me, God, and know my heart; test me and know my anxious thoughts. See if there is any offensive way in me, and lead me in the way everlasting" (NIV).

. . . . **Praise** . . . .

Lord I praise You that You are the God Who
Hears. You listen to my prayers and concerns, and
never withdraw Your unfailing love from me.

· · · · · · · · · · · · · · · · Confession · · · · · · · · · · · · · · · · ·

Lord, please forgive me for the sin I cling to. Help me to release it to You and not hold onto it or take it back.

· · · · · · · · · · · · · · Thanksgiving · · · · · · · · · · · · · ·

May I remember to tell others what You did for me. Lord, I thank You specifically for...

· · · · · · · · · · · · · · · · Intercession · · · · · · · · · · · · · · · ·

Lord, as You did for me, I pray that You will help _____ confess the sin in his/her heart, so that You will hear his/her prayers.

· · · · · · · · · · · · · · · · Petition · · · · · · · · · · · · · · · · · · ·

Lord, search me and show me my anxious thoughts and offensive ways. Forgive me and lead me in Your everlasting way.

From Psalm 139:23-24

12

Stop Pushing God Away

> *When Simon Peter saw that, he fell down at Jesus's*
> *feet, saying, "Go away from me Lord, for I am a*
> *sinful man!"...And Jesus said to Simon, "Do not*
> *fear, from now on you will be catching men."*

LUKE 5:8,10

*a*fter we truly see who God is, it brings us to our knees! When you spent the first 10 days of this devotional in praise reflecting on God, did it bring you to your knees and open your heart to confess your sins?

Notice what Jesus tells Peter to do when he falls at Jesus's feet, weighed down by his sin. Jesus directs him not to fear. Peter would learn to trust Jesus enough to surrender his sins and his life to Him. God had something great in store for Peter—something greater than what this world could give him!

Isaiah had a moment like Peter when he was face-to-face with God. God was about to work through Him powerfully, yet Isaiah had to come to the end of himself. Isaiah would need to confess his sin so God could move in and through him powerfully.

> In the year of King Uzziah's death I saw the Lord sitting on a throne, lofty and exalted, with the train of His robe filling the temple. Seraphim stood above Him, each having six wings: with two he covered his face, and with two

73

he covered his feet, and with two he flew. And one called out to another and said,

> "Holy, Holy, Holy, is the LORD of hosts,
> The whole earth is full of His glory."

And the foundations of the thresholds trembled at the voice of him who called out, while the temple was filling with smoke. Then I said,

> "Woe is me, for I am ruined!
>> Because I am a man of unclean lips,
> And I live among a people of unclean lips;
>> For my eyes have seen the King,
>> the LORD of hosts."

Then one of the seraphim flew to me with a burning coal in his hand, which he had taken from the altar with tongs. He touched my mouth with it and said, "Behold, this has touched your lips; and your iniquity is taken away and your sin is forgiven." Then I heard the voice of the Lord, saying, "Whom shall I send, and who will go for Us?" Then I said, "Here am I. Send me!" (Isaiah 6:1-8).

Oh, can't we relate to the unclean lips! How easy our words can slip out. Our words can bring great harm to others and ourselves. Our words can glorify God and His work, or destroy one another and defile His name.

James 3:5-12

See how great a forest is set aflame by such a small fire! And the tongue is a fire, the very world of iniquity; the tongue is set among our members as that which defiles the entire body, and sets on fire the course of our life, and is set on fire by hell. For every species of beasts and birds, of reptiles and creatures of the sea, is tamed and has been

tamed by the human race. But no one can tame the
tongue; it is a restless evil and full of deadly poison. With
it we bless our Lord and Father, and with it we curse men,
who have been made in the likeness of God; from the
same mouth come both blessing and cursing. My brethren, these things ought not to be this way. Does a foun-
tain send out from the same opening both fresh and
bitter water? Can a fig tree, my brethren, produce olives,
or a vine produce figs? Nor can salt water produce fresh.

Remember Christ's disciple Peter whose words had him in trouble
often? One minute, Peter is speaking God's words (Matthew 16:15-17)
and the next he is rebuking Jesus (Matthew 16:22-23). He did both
with the same tongue. And yet Jesus was not going to leave Peter there.
He was going to make Peter a man who, with God's words, would
bring thousands to salvation and glory to God.

Our imperfections do not stop God's work through us, but unconfessed sin will. We cannot hide our sin or talk our way around it. But
we can use our words to confess our sins and allow Him to complete
what He has begun in us.

2 Corinthians 3:18

We all, with unveiled face, beholding as in a mirror the
glory of the Lord, are being transformed into the same
image from glory to glory, just as from the Lord, the Spirit.

Just as God was in the process of sanctifying Peter and Isaiah, He's
doing the same for you and me. God's words have the power to sanctify us, set us apart for a greater work than we can imagine. Use your
words to confess your sins, so you can hear His words and hear His
calling on your life.

John 17:17 says, "Sanctify them in the truth; Your word is truth."
Jesus prayed this for us before He went to the cross to cover our sins
with His blood. And His word continues to flow through us. "For the

word of God is living and active and sharper than any two-edged sword, and piercing as far as the division of soul and spirit, of both joints and marrow, and able to judge the thoughts and intentions of the heart" (Hebrews 4:12).

* *

Use your words to confess your sins, so you can
hear His words and hear His calling on your life.

* *

Before we move on, I have an important question for you. Do you truly belong to God? God will invest in you all of Himself if you belong to Him. He will remodel you from the inside out, from glory to glory into His image. You will be a beautiful house for His Spirit to dwell in!

I remember when I became God's child. I was like Peter when I first saw who Jesus is. I was reading the gospel of John. It was there I met God. It was there I knew Jesus was God. But instead of telling Jesus to go away from me, I invited Him in. I received His free gift of salvation.

Ephesians 2:4-5,8-10

God, being rich in mercy, because of His great love with which He loved us, even when we were dead in our transgressions, made us alive together with Christ... For by grace you have been saved through faith; and that not of yourselves, it is the gift of God; not as a result of works, so that no one may boast. For we are His workmanship, created in Christ Jesus for good works, which God prepared beforehand so that we would walk in them.

If you have not received Jesus as Lord and Savior, accept His free gift of salvation and let the greatest remodeling begin. Allow Him to clean you from the inside out so His light shines through you, so you can be truly empowered by Christ!

Praise

For the Mighty One is holy,
and he has done great things for me.
He shows mercy from generation to generation
to all who fear him.

LUKE 1:49-50

Confession

Woe is me, for I am ruined! Because I am a man/woman
of unclean lips, and I live among a people of unclean
lips; for my eyes have seen the King, the LORD of hosts.

FROM ISAIAH 6:5

Thanksgiving

Lord, thank You that I can draw near with confidence
to the throne of grace, so that I may receive mercy
and find grace to help in time of need.

FROM HEBREWS 4:16

Intercession

Let the words of _____'s mouth and the
meditation of his/her heart be acceptable in Your
sight, O LORD, our rock and our Redeemer.

FROM PSALM 19:14

• • • • • • • • • • • • • • • • • • • **Petition** • • • • • • • • • • • • • • • • • •

Let the words of my mouth and the meditation of my heart be
acceptable in Your sight, O LORD, my rock and my Redeemer.

FROM PSALM 19:14

13

Do We Really Love One Another?

.... Cyndie ....

*Dear friends, let us continue to love one another, for
love comes from God. Anyone who loves is a child
of God and knows God. But anyone who does
not love does not know God, for God is love.*

1 JOHN 4:7-8 NLT

How are you at loving others? Usually, if we're keeping our eyes on the Lord and spending time in His Word and praying, love for others flows out of us as naturally as the water rushes down the Niagara Falls. But when our focus shifts off God and onto ourselves, well, that makes loving others a chore. We become defensive and easily offended. We worry that someone else's good news might actually be bad news for us. We complain and get angry. *Love others? Why? What have they done for me?*

Which category do you fall into? Is God's love overflowing from your life onto others, or would it be hard to know you're a Christian from the way you treat others?

Remember, God doesn't require us to do anything in our own strength, especially loving others. Our own meager attempts might feel shallow and selfish, but love empowered through God's strength is genuine, compelling, and glorifies our Creator.

The beauty of confession is that it's simple and complete. All we have to do is come before our heavenly Father, admit the sin, and ask for His forgiveness. He will always—one hundred percent of the time—forgive us. Always. Then we can ask Him to empower us, to be our strength in our weakness.

Sharing God's love with others is the hallmark of Christianity. But that doesn't mean it's easy. As you read through 1 Corinthians 13, ask God in which areas you fall short. Confess that as sin, then ask Him to fill you with His love to overflowing, and focus on those areas. It might help to memorize the particular verse or phrase where God is working in your life.

> If I could speak all the languages of earth and of angels, but didn't love others, I would only be a noisy gong or a clanging cymbal. If I had the gift of prophecy, and if I understood all of God's secret plans and possessed all knowledge, and if I had such faith that I could move mountains, but didn't love others, I would be nothing. If I gave everything I have to the poor and even sacrificed my body, I could boast about it; but if I didn't love others, I would have gained nothing.
>
> Love is patient and kind. Love is not jealous or boastful or proud or rude. It does not demand its own way. It is not irritable, and it keeps no record of being wronged. It does not rejoice about injustice but rejoices whenever the truth wins out. Love never gives up, never loses faith, is always hopeful, and endures through every circumstance... Three things will last forever—faith, hope, and love—and the greatest of these is love (1 Corinthians 13:1-7,13 NLT).

· · · · · · · · · · · · · · · · · · · **Praise** · · · · · · · · · · · · · · · · · · ·

Lord, I praise You for being the God of love. You loved the world so much that You sent Your only son to die for us. That love is so amazing!

• • • • • • • • • • • • • • • • Confession • • • • • • • • • • • • • • • •

Lord, please forgive me for not always sharing Your love with others. Forgive me for the times I am selfish, impatient, jealous, boastful, or rude. Help me to be able to forgive others as You forgive me. Empower me to never give up, never lose faith and always be hopeful and endure through every circumstance. I can't do this in my own strength, Lord. Empty me of my self-centered ways, and help me to see others as You do, through the eyes of love.

• • • • • • • • • • • • • • • • Thanksgiving • • • • • • • • • • • • • • • •

Lord, I thank You for the times that You have helped me love when I was not feeling very loving. Specifically, Lord, I thank You for...

• • • • • • • • • • • • • • • • Intercession • • • • • • • • • • • • • • • •

Lord, help _____ to be so overwhelmed with Your love that he/she wants to pour out Your love on others. I pray that You will help _____ be patient and kind; to not be jealous or boastful or rude. Help _____ not demand his/her own way, not be irritable, and not keep records of being wronged. May he/she not rejoice in injustice but rejoice when the truth wins out. Help _____ never give up or lose faith, but instead be hopeful always and enduring through every circumstance.

FROM 1 CORINTHIANS 13

· · · · · · · · · · · · · · · · · · · **Petition** · · · · · · · · · · · · · · · · · ·

Lord, help me love like You, as 1 Corinthians 13 says. Help me be so overwhelmed with Your love that I want to pour out Your love on others. I pray that You will help me be patient and kind; to not be jealous or boastful or rude. Help me not demand my own way, not be irritable, and not keep records of being wronged. May I not rejoice in injustice but rejoice when the truth wins out. Help me never give up or lose faith, but instead be hopeful always and enduring through every circumstance.

FROM 1 CORINTHIANS 13

14

Forgive as the Father Forgives Us

· · · · · · · · · · · · · · · · · · Sally ·

But Jesus was saying, "Father, forgive them; for
they do not know what they are doing."

LUKE 23:34

*Y*ou may have read in our book *Unshaken* the story of our dear sister from Rwanda, who suffered the loss of two children who were killed. Through Christ's empowerment in her life, she was able to forgive those in Rwanda who killed her children. After she had moved to America, the power of forgiveness freed her to return to Rwanda. She even brought her other children with her to share the love of God with the people there.

She could have let her unforgiveness and fear hold her back. Instead, her forgiveness set her free and allowed her to impact the people and the country that took so much from her. When she returned to Rwanda, she taught many people how to pray for one another instead of fighting and killing. She was teaching them how to give a future and a hope to this next generation. Because she learned how to forgive, she was able to move forward, empowered to impact a nation through prayer.

Matthew 18:21-35

Then Peter came and said to Him, "Lord, how often shall my brother sin against me and I forgive him? Up to seven times?" Jesus said to him, "I do not say to you, up to seven times, but up to seventy times seven.

"For this reason the kingdom of heaven may be compared to a king who wished to settle accounts with his slaves. When he had begun to settle them, one who owed him ten thousand talents was brought to him. But since he did not have the means to repay, his lord commanded him to be sold, along with his wife and children and all that he had, and repayment to be made. So the slave fell to the ground and prostrated himself before him, saying, 'Have patience with me and I will repay you everything.' And the lord of that slave felt compassion and released him and forgave him the debt. But that slave went out and found one of his fellow slaves who owed him a hundred denarii; and he seized him and began to choke him, saying, 'Pay back what you owe.' So his fellow slave fell to the ground and began to plead with him, saying, 'Have patience with me and I will repay you.' But he was unwilling and went and threw him in prison until he should pay back what was owed. So when his fellow slaves saw what had happened, they were deeply grieved and came and reported to their lord all that had happened. Then summoning him, his lord said to him, 'You wicked slave, I forgave you all that debt because you pleaded with me. Should you not also have had mercy on your fellow slave, in the same way that I had mercy on you?' And his lord, moved with anger, handed him over to the torturers until he should repay all that was owed him. My heavenly Father will also do the same to you, if each of you does not forgive his brother from your heart."

God has forgiven you and me of all our sins! He paid the price with His own Son, His own blood. God remembers our sins no more! The parable above talks about being handed over to the torturers. When we do not forgive, we allow the torture of unforgiveness to eat at our souls.

Matthew 6:14-15

> For if you forgive others for their transgressions, your heavenly Father will also forgive you. But if you do not forgive others, then your Father will not forgive your transgressions.

Sometimes the hardest person to forgive is ourselves! Many of us think, *If I could have, should have, or would have done things differently all my troubles would be washed away.* We see our past with 20-20 vision. We all make mistakes but must forgive ourselves and allow God to lead us forward. Even though "we are faithless, He remains faithful, for He cannot deny Himself" (2 Timothy 2:13). So the truth is that once you go to Him to repent of your sins, you must forgive yourself. You do not want to give control to the enemy of your soul.

One woman I know admittedly shared how she hated her son for what he had done to their family through his addictions. She was also angry with herself for what she had allowed. She needed to forgive both her son and herself. She needed to release her son to the Lord. She could not fix him, nor did she have power over the situation.

....

We all make mistakes but must forgive
ourselves and allow God to lead us forward.

....

Yet as she forgave him and herself, she was able to release her son to the Lord. It was then that God unleashed His power to help her son. Now, her son is doing amazingly well. He is reunited with the family, and they both are pointing many to God.

Let us not hold back the hand of God with our unforgiveness. Let us not miss out on what God wants to do through us as we pray.

These words in Luke 23:34 came from Jesus who had no sin, who was beaten beyond recognition, spit upon, yelled at, and hung on a cross dying for our sins: "Father, forgive them; for they do not know what they are doing."

When someone hurts me, I try to remember right away to say the same words as Christ. If I do, the sin of unforgiveness does not take root. I am not sinless, I am not perfect like Jesus is, but if He can say those words, then I can. And then God sets me free and empowers me to forgive.

Are you ready to set your soul free of unforgiveness and move forward? Let's start right now!

· · · · · · · · · · · · · · · · · · **Praise** · · · · · · · · · · · · · · · · · ·

Day and night I will not cease to say "Holy, holy, holy is the Lord God, the Almighty, who was and who is and who is to come."

FROM REVELATION 4:8

Lord, I praise You for You alone are perfect and holy.

· · · · · · · · · · · · · · · · · · **Confession** · · · · · · · · · · · · · · · · ·

Lord help me to forgive _____ for they do not know what they are doing.

· · · · · · · · · · · · · · · · · · **Thanksgiving** · · · · · · · · · · · · · · · ·

Lord, thank You for all the times You have forgiven me and that You remember my sins no longer.

· · · · · · · · · · · · · · · · · · **Intercession** · · · · · · · · · · · · · · · · · ·

Lord, help _____ be on his/her guard! If someone sins against him/her, help _____ to rebuke that person in love, and if the person repents, help him/her to forgive them. And if the person sins against him/her seven times a day and returns to him/her seven times, saying "I repent," help _____ to forgive that person.

FROM LUKE 17:3-4

· · · · · · · · · · · · · · · · · · **Petition** · · · · · · · · · · · · · · · · · ·

Lord, help me be on guard! If someone sins against me, help me rebuke him/her in love; and if the person repents, help me forgive him/her. And if the person sins against me seven times a day, and returns to me seven times, saying, "I repent," help me forgive that person.

FROM LUKE 17:3-4

15

Let the God of Peace Cleanse You

.... Cyndie ....

*May God himself, the God of peace, sanctify you through
and through. May your whole spirit, soul and body be
kept blameless at the coming of our Lord Jesus Christ.
The one who calls you is faithful, and he will do it.*

1 Thessalonians 5:23-24 niv

Do you crave a deep relationship with your Creator? Do you want
to experience the peace that comes from being clean and sanctified before God?

First Thessalonians 5 is a great chapter to pray through, asking Him
to show you any sin that you might be dabbling in before you are fully
entrenched and drowning in it. Review these verses 12-24, asking the
Lord to show you any areas you need to confess before Him.

> We ask you, brothers and sisters, to acknowledge those
> who work hard among you, who care for you in the
> Lord and who admonish you. Hold them in the high-
> est regard in love because of their work. Live in peace
> with each other. And we urge you, brothers and sisters,
> warn those who are idle and disruptive, encourage the
> disheartened, help the weak, be patient with everyone.
> Make sure that nobody pays back wrong for wrong, but
> always strive to do what is good for each other and for
> everyone else.

> Rejoice always, pray continually, give thanks in all circumstances; for this is God's will for you in Christ Jesus.
>
> Do not quench the Spirit. Do not treat prophecies with contempt but test them all; hold on to what is good, reject every kind of evil.
>
> May God himself, the God of peace, sanctify you through and through. May your whole spirit, soul and body be kept blameless at the coming of our Lord Jesus Christ. The one who calls you is faithful, and he will do it (NIV).

Here's the most amazing thing: We do not even have to confess in our own strength. God helps us, not just by convicting us but also by cleansing us. According to 1 Thessalonians 5, who is sanctifying us? God. Not us! We only need to repent of our sins and allow God to fully restore our relationship with Him. Psalm 51:7 says, "Cleanse me with hyssop, and I will be clean; wash me, and I will be whiter than snow" (NIV). Who is doing the cleaning? Our heavenly Father!

Now look at Psalm 139:23-24, "Search me, God, and know my heart; test me and know my anxious thoughts. See if there is any offensive way in me, and lead me in the way everlasting" (NIV). David didn't try to cleanse himself or search his own thoughts. He asked God to do that. Only the Holy God who is free from sin can truly cleanse us.

The description of God in 1 Thessalonians 5:23-24 is "the God of peace." His goal isn't to rip open old wounds and let us hemorrhage uncontrollably. He doesn't want to flog us and cause us to verbally lash ourselves in faux humility. He wants us to allow Him to lovingly search our hearts, to cleanse us and to sanctify us through and through.

Will you let Him do this for you?

 **Praise**

Lord, we praise You for being the God of peace who desires to cleanse us and have a relationship with us.

Confession

*Lord, forgive me for the times that I don't esteem those
in my church. Forgive me for my part in not living
at peace with _____. Forgive me, too, for
the times that I am not thankful and forget to praise
You. Lord, I pray that You will forgive me for...*

Thanksgiving

*You are the Almighty One, yet You choose to forgive our sins
each and every time we confess them to You. Lord, I so thank
You for that. I specifically thank You for forgiving me for...*

Intercession

*Lord, help _____ strive to do what is good for others.
Help him/her rejoice in You always, to remember to pray
continually, to give thanks in all circumstances; for this is Your
will for us. I also pray that _____ will not quench Your
Spirit. Help him/her hold on to what is good and reject every
kind of evil. Lord, You are the God of peace. Please sanctify
_____ through and through, keeping his/her spirit, soul,
and body blameless. Help him/her know that You called him/
her, and You are faithful to accomplish Your will through us.*

FROM 1 THESSALONIANS 5:15-24

······················· Petition ··················

Lord, help me strive to do what is good for others. Help me rejoice in You always, to remember to pray continually, to give thanks in all circumstances; for this is Your will for me. Help me also not to quench Your Spirit. Help me hold on to what is good and reject every kind of evil. Lord, You are the God of peace. Please sanctify me through and through, keeping my spirit, soul, and body blameless. Help me remember that You called me, and You are faithful to accomplish Your will through me.

FROM 1 THESSALONIANS 5:15-24

16

Confession Brings Rest and Refreshment

· Sally ·

Come to Me, all who are weary and heavy-laden,
and I will give you rest. Take My yoke upon you
and learn from Me, for I am gentle and humble in
heart, and YOU WILL FIND REST FOR YOUR SOULS.

MATTHEW 11:28-29

*H*olding on to our sins wears us out, brings us down, entangles us and ultimately can destroy us and our loved ones.

I think King David describes well the burden of holding on to our sins. Below are his words before the confession of his sins. His whole body felt the crushing pressure that hidden sin brings, demonstrating what happens when sin goes further than you ever imagine, beyond our own intentions or solutions.

> There is no soundness in my flesh
>   because of Your indignation;
> There is no health in my bones because of my sin.
> For my iniquities are gone over my head;
> As a heavy burden they weigh too much for me.
> My wounds grow foul and fester because of my folly.
> I am bent over and greatly bowed down;
> I go mourning all day long.
> For my loins are filled with burning,
> And there is no soundness in my flesh.

> I am benumbed and badly crushed;
> I groan because of the agitation of my heart
> (Psalm 38:3-8).

King David, a man after God's own heart, tried to cover his sin, which only led to lies, murder, and his entire family and nation being stricken with trouble. Yet God came to David so David could confess his sins and be free. At the end of his life, King David was a leader who was highly respected and was able to impact God's children for generations to come.

At Moms in Prayer International headquarters we receive so many stories of young prodigals who are exhausted from drugs, alcohol, lifestyle choices, lies, and all that sin brings. They tell us they are weary, even to the point of lying on the floor and not being able to lift their bodies from the ground. They wish to die so the pain, suffering, and bondage created by their sin will stop.

It is there they come to the end of themselves. It is there they call upon God, who has always been there, and hears and answers their prayers! Once they confess to God their sins and ask Him for help, He empowers them to the fullness of freedom.

The picture of the prodigal son in the Bible always touches me. The father is waiting for the son to return and comes running to the prodigal as the prodigal turns from his sin and heads back to the father. Read below and see how Jesus describes it.

> So he [the prodigal son] got up and came to his father. But while he was still a long way off, his father saw him and felt compassion for him, and ran and embraced him and kissed him. And the son said to him, "Father, I have sinned against heaven and in your sight; I am no longer worthy to be called your son." But the father said to his slaves, "Quickly bring out the best robe and put it on him, and put a ring on his hand and sandals on his feet; and bring the fattened calf, kill it, and let us eat and celebrate; for this son of mine was dead and has come to life

again; he was lost and has been found." And they began
to celebrate (Luke 15:20-24).

The moms I know who have prodigals never give up. They persevere in prayer for them, even when it's hard or a positive answer seems
impossible. Romans 8:34 says, "Who is the one who condemns? Christ
Jesus is He who died, yes, rather who was raised, who is at the right
hand of God, who also intercedes for us." You and I have Jesus praying for us, and He never quits. "Therefore He is able also to save forever those who draw near to God through Him, since He always lives
to make intercession for them" (Hebrews 7:25).

Now you may say you're not a prodigal or have never sinned like
King David, but any sin will have lasting effect and bondage. We must
confess and repent any sin that entangles or hinders us.

It's not hard to tell if we are holding onto sin, is it? When we are
downtrodden, weary, lacking joy, we might be in desperate need for
the heavy burden of a sin to be lifted by the Lord.

Take it to Jesus. Jesus came to free us from our sins!

Matthew 9:12-13

When Jesus heard this, He said, "It is not those who are
healthy who need a physician, but those who are sick.
But go and learn what this means: 'I DESIRE COMPAS-
SION, AND NOT SACRIFICE,' for I did not come to call the
righteous, but sinners."

Jesus not only died for the penalty of our sins, but to defeat the hold
they have in our lives. We must confess our sins and repent of them so
we can find rest for our souls.

· ·

Take it to Jesus.

· ·

According to the *Easton Bible Dictionary*, the definition of true repentance includes "a true sense of one's own guilt and sinfulness" and a "turning from it to God." You and I get to turn away from the ugliness and destruction of our sins and turn toward Jesus. What we will see is the beautiful loving face of our Savior and the refreshment for our souls!

Come. Come find rest for your weary soul.

· · · · · · · · · · · · · · · · · · Praise · · · · · · · · · · · · · · · · · ·

Lord, You are our Savior who can save us completely. You are waiting with loving arms open wide to receive us to Yourself. You always live to intercede for us! I praise You, Lord.

· · · · · · · · · · · · · · · · · Confession · · · · · · · · · · · · · · · · ·

Lord, the weight of my sin is too much for me to carry. Today, I confess...

And I repent and turn to You!

· · · · · · · · · · · · · · · Thanksgiving · · · · · · · · · · · · · · · · ·

Lord, thank You so much for carrying my burden, for giving me rest for my weary soul.

· · · · · · · · · · · · · · · · · **Intercession** · · · · · · · · · · · · · · · · ·

*Jesus, help_____ remain in Your love, obeying Your commands,
so that he/she will be filled with Your joy to overflowing!*

FROM JOHN 15:10–11

· · · · · · · · · · · · · · · · · **Petition** · · · · · · · · · · · · · · · · · ·

*Jesus, help me remain in Your love, obeying Your commands,
so that I will be filled with Your joy to overflowing. You
command me to give You my burdens so You can give me
rest for my soul. Please help me follow that command, to
hand You my burdens and not pick them back up again.*

FROM JOHN 15:10-11 AND MATTHEW 11:28-29

17

Giving God Our Worries

· · · · · · · · · · · · · · · · · Cyndie · · · · · · · · · · · · · · · · ·

Cast all your anxiety on him because he cares for you.

1 Peter 5:7 NIV

*B*eing anxious often feels like a natural part of life. After all, when we push our way into the world, we're already surrounded by worry. For many people, when children enter their lives, so does a constant stream of anxiety and fears. Are they eating enough? Are they eating too much? Did we choose the right school? Sports? Activities? Are they too busy? Or are they not busy enough? Will they ever be responsible enough to be on their own? Should they be on their own?

Worry and anxiety feel like just a part of being human, right? Yet, God tells us to hand over all our anxiety, worries, and fears to Him. Why? Because He loves and cares for us. In fact, Philippians 4 tells us that He'll exchange all those blood-pressure raising concerns with peace, if we just hand them over to Him.

> Do not be anxious about anything, but in every situation, by prayer and petition, with thanksgiving, present your requests to God. And the peace of God, which transcends all understanding, will guard your hearts and your minds in Christ Jesus (Philippians 4:6-7 NIV).

As much as we might want to hand over our anxiety to God in exchange for His peace, it can be extremely difficult to do so.

I was pondering these verses as I was sitting between my husband and daughter on an airplane headed to our dream vacation—a week at Walt Disney World. The only slight cause for concern was that my college-student son was flying separately and meeting us there. As our plane took to the sky, my mind was beginning to spin an elaborate web of worry.

The morning before our departure to Florida, I had enjoyed a lovely time with the Lord and felt completely at peace about our adventure. Of course, that was easy while sitting in my comfy quiet-time chair. But, at this moment, strapped into my airplane seat, flying high above the ground, my mind was racing with what-ifs. What if my 19-year-old son couldn't find the right airline at the airport—again? What if he brought his whole tube of toothpaste—again—and was detained because, you know, it could look like a bomb, or something. Plus, the news was dotted with terrorist attacks around the globe, and I was most worried that my son, with his light brown skin, hair, and eyes, and sporting a trimmed beard and mustache, might be mistaken as, well, you know, a possible terrorist. I mean, a young adult male traveling alone... isn't that one of the profiles that security looks for? As the worry fed itself, growing bigger and bigger, it crescendoed into one more final fear: How would I even know if he was detained, since I was strapped to the seat of an airplane!

As I was making mental leaps to the worst-case scenarios, God gently reminded me of Philippians 4:6-7. My fretting was overriding my faith, peace, contentment, and joy. It was time to confess. So, sitting on the plane, between my husband watching one movie and my daughter watching another, I took a deep breath, exhaling slowly, and began to pray silently:

> Lord, I praise You that You are all-knowing and all-powerful, and that You orchestrate all things together for good, as You promise in Romans 8:28. I'm sorry that I'm not trusting You. Of course, You can get Elliott on the right plane to meet us at the right time. Please forgive me of this sin of worry. Please help me to give You

this anxiety, so I can experience Your peace. Thank You that I can trust your promises. Thank You that we can take this amazing trip. Thank You that Elliott was brave enough to fly by himself. Thank You for the many pieces You put into place to even make this trip possible. And, thank You, Lord, for loving my son even more than I do—which really doesn't seem possible.

And, guess what happened? God forgave me. And, as is promised in Philippians 4, if we hand over our worry to God, He replaces it with peace. And each time I went to worry, the Holy Spirit tugged at my heart, and I confessed all over again.

Why do I share this somewhat mundane story with you? To drive home the point that confession is daily—and sometimes several times a day. Confession is clearing the channel between you and God to allow for direct communication with the One who created the entire universe, the One who has a specific plan for you and for each of your loved ones.

> If we hand over our worry to God,
> He replaces it with peace.

Do you want to experience His inexplicable peace? Confess your sin of worry, and let the Holy Spirit bathe you in His peace.

Praise

Lord, I praise You that You love and care for us, and that You promise to exchange our fears, worries, and anxieties for Your inexplicable peace.

·················· Confession ··················

Lord, it is so hard to release my anxiety to You. Please forgive me for each time I begin fretting over things out of my control, as well as for the ones that are within my control. Remind me every time to confess my sin of worry, fear, and anxiety, and to pry my hands off my concerns and to place them in Your more-than-capable hands.

·················· Thanksgiving ··················

Lord, thank You for taking care of my concerns and working them together for good. Specifically, I thank You for...

·················· Intercession ··················

I pray that _____ will cast all his/her anxiety on You because You care for_____.

From 1 Peter 5:7

·················· Petition ··················

Lord, every time my mind clings to the what-ifs, help me to cast all my fears, worries, and concerns onto You. Give me the conviction and peace to trust that You care about me and my family and friends even more than I do, and You will weave each piece together for Your good purpose.

From 1 Peter 5:7 and Romans 8:28

18

Confessing Our Anger

·················· Sally ····················

*But I tell you that anyone who is angry with a
brother or sister will be subject to judgment. Again,
anyone who says to a brother or sister, "Raca," is
answerable to the court. And anyone who says, "You
fool!" will be in danger of the fire of hell.*

MATTHEW 5:22 NIV

*S*ometimes I get so mad at my husband that I will take my Bible
and go upstairs to pray for him. I think he needs prayer. I think
God needs to fix *him*. You may not be angry with your husband but
maybe you are angry with a friend, a relative, or a co-worker. Perhaps
your anger is directed at your situation or the way the world is heading. Do you get so angry that you could hate others or wish them the
worst or call them fools?

We see so much evidence of anger today. Anger that turns to vio-
lence—that destroys families, churches, nations. Even at the risk of
such destruction, many people still hold onto their anger and hate. We
may think it is righteous anger or believe that we know exactly what
God needs to do to fix the situation. We may try, as Sarah in the Old
Testament did, to manipulate the situation in the direction we think is
best, only to find out we made a complete mess of everyone's life.

You can read in Genesis 16 the story that seems to be meant for a
soap opera, not for a woman of faith. Yet Sarah is considered a woman
of great faith. Hebrews 11:11 says, "By faith even Sarah herself received

ability to conceive, even beyond the proper time of life, since she considered Him faithful who had promised." She had to learn to let go of her anger, her wants, her ways and surrender them to God. Then God gave her the desires of her heart. In Psalm 37:4 God tells us, "Delight yourself in the LORD, and He will give you the desires of your heart."

God had work to do in Sarah's heart. And He has work to do in our hearts. What can we do to avoid taking our anger to the next level—or our needs above those of another? How can God take a heart that is "more deceitful than all else and is desperately sick" (Jeremiah 17:9) and make it pure?

When I'm angry with my husband, I have learned to head upstairs in my house and spend time before the Lord. When I'm alone with God, even if I start off angry, God begins to speak to my heart as I open up His Word and begin to pray. He shows me where I have gone astray. He reveals what I need to confess. Before I know it, I am heading back downstairs with a joy-filled, loving heart toward my husband. I ask him to forgive me if I have done anything wrong. I am totally free of anger, hatred, frustration, or anything that pulls me away from God and others. And you should see the look on my husband's face! He may not repent or ask for my forgiveness, and that is okay. I pray he will, but I must trust God in leading him as God has led me toward freedom.

I became so rehearsed in this process that I could discern when I was about to give myself over to anger and frustration. I would tell my kids that Mommy had to take a minute and be with Jesus so I would not blow out anger at them. I would go and talk with Jesus and come back. Before I knew it, my kids could tell when I was about to lose it and say, "Mommy you need to go be with Jesus."

We must know this truth that our battle is not against people. The enemy would love to destroy our peace, our relationships, our families, and our future. Ephesians 6:12 says, "Our struggle is not against flesh and blood, but against the rulers, against the authorities, against the powers of this dark world and against the spiritual forces of evil in the heavenly realms" (NIV).

Our spouse, friends, or co-workers could be wrong, and we could have righteous anger; yet, it can lead us to sin. Ephesians 4:26 says, "In your anger do not sin: Do not let the sun go down while you are still angry" (NIV). How many times have you allowed unfairness or past wrongs to get the best of you and weigh you down? As someone said to me: When you let anger, bitterness, hatred get ahold of your heart it is like taking poison that you wish the other person was taking. If anger, bitterness, hatred take ahold of our hearts, we die inside and then we are ugly outside.

But God can bring us peace, restoration, victory, and power over our anger and the other person's hold on us. Even if we live in the same house or work together. God can raise us above it. We know what to do.

Hebrews 12:14-15

> Pursue peace with all men, and the sanctification with-
> out which no one will see the Lord. See to it that no one
> comes short of the grace of God; that no root of bitterness
> springing up causes trouble, and by it many be defiled.

As I confess my sins, whatever they may be—wrong thinking, anger, hatred, sinful desires, wanting harm for another—God forgives me and replaces these sins with His agape love, inexpressible joy, peace beyond all understanding, patience to wait for His best outcome, and all the fruit of the Spirit can be mine. God will deal with the other person; our part is to stay pure and pray for the other person.

So let us take all our anger, hatred, and resentment of others to our Jesus...and we can exchange the ugliness of our hearts for the beauty of the Lord's heart!

· · · · · · · · · · · · · · · · · **Praise** · · · · · · · · · · · · · · · · · ·

Lord I praise You that You are the God of love. "For God so loved
the world, that He gave His only begotten Son, that whoever
believes in Him shall not perish, but have eternal life. For God
did not send the Son into the world to judge the world, but
that the world might be saved through Him" (John 3:16-17).

· · · · · · · · · · · · · · Confession · · · · · · · · · · · · · ·

*Forgive me for my anger, hatred and whatever I am
feeling against _____. You call me to love
my enemies and to love others as I love myself.*

· · · · · · · · · · · · · Thanksgiving · · · · · · · · · · · · · ·

*Thank You, Lord, that Your Holy Spirit lives in me. You have
empowered me to turn my anger and wrath into loving others.*

· · · · · · · · · · · · · · Intercession · · · · · · · · · · · · · ·

Help _____ love others, for love is from You.

From 1 John 4:7

· · · · · · · · · · · · · · Petition · · · · · · · · · · · · · ·

Lord, help me love others, for love is from You.

From 1 John 4:7

19

What Am I Focusing On?

· · · · · · · · · · · · · · · · · · Cyndie · · · · · · · · · · · · · · · · · ·

*Since, then, you have been raised with Christ, set your hearts on
things above, where Christ is, seated at the right hand of God. Set
your minds on things above, not on earthly things. For you died,
and your life is now hidden with Christ in God. When Christ, who
is your life, appears, then you also will appear with him in glory.*

*Put to death, therefore, whatever belongs to your earthly nature:
sexual immorality, impurity, lust, evil desires and greed, which is
idolatry. Because of these, the wrath of God is coming. You used to
walk in these ways, in the life you once lived. But now you must also
rid yourselves of all such things as these: anger, rage, malice, slander,
and filthy language from your lips. Do not lie to each other, since you
have taken off your old self with its practices and have put on the new
self, which is being renewed in knowledge in the image of its Creator.
Here there is no Gentile or Jew, circumcised or uncircumcised,
barbarian, Scythian, slave or free, but Christ is all, and is in all.*

*Therefore, as God's chosen people, holy and dearly loved, clothe
yourselves with compassion, kindness, humility, gentleness
and patience. Bear with each other and forgive one another
if any of you has a grievance against someone. Forgive as
the Lord forgave you. And over all these virtues put on
love, which binds them all together in perfect unity.*

Colossians 3:1-14 niv

*I*n high school, I memorized the book of Colossians so I could earn a free trip to our church summer camp. What I didn't realize at the time was that I was getting much more than a week at camp. Psalm 119:11 says, "I have hidden your word in my heart that I might not sin against you" (NIV). Oh, how true it was for me after I had committed Colossians 3 into my heart. As a teen, whether I worried about tests, or boys, or my car puttering out on the freeway, the scriptures reminded me to set my mind on things above rather than on earthly things.

When I can't stop ruminating over a concern, God uses His Word that's hidden in my heart to remind me that if I keep my eyes on Him, the rest of the truths that fill the chapter—and all of the Bible—fall in line, so that I can be empowered by the Holy Spirit. With that focus, let's take an inventory and ask God what to confess. Review the Colossians verses again. Then look at the list below. What is the Holy Spirit convicting you of? Spend time praying through each one and asking the Lord to search your heart and uncover what part of the "earthly nature" do you need to "put to death" in the name of Jesus Christ.

- Sexual immorality
- Impurity
- Lust
- Evil desires
- Greed
- Anger
- Rage
- Malice
- Slander / Gossip
- Filthy language
- Lying

Now, circle the area you feel the Holy Spirit is calling you to work on in His power and strength:

- Compassion
- Kindness
- Humility

- Gentleness
- Patience
- Bearing with / supporting each other
- Forgiving others
- Showing God's love
- Encouraging unity

Now, confess those sins and ask the Lord to help you in each of these areas. But remember the first part of Colossians 3. Oh, how easy it is to lose sight of Christ and focus only on our sin and shortcomings. But that is *not* what we're called to do. Colossians 3:2-3 commands: "Set your minds on things above, not on earthly things. For you died, and your life is now hidden with Christ in God" (NIV). Meditate on these verses until they permeate your heart. As you focus on Christ—and not your shortcomings—His characteristics will begin to shine through you.

· · · · · · · · · · · · · · · · · **Praise** · · · · · · · · · · · · · · · · · ·

Colossians 3:13 says, "Forgive as the Lord forgave you" (NIV). Lord, I praise You that You are a God of forgiveness. Psalm 103:12 promises, "As far as the east is from the west, so far has he removed our transgressions from us" (NIV). Lord, I'm amazed that You who are holy can also be so forgiving of humankind—of myself, especially. My sins have been erased by the blood of Jesus Christ. I so praise You for that!

· · · · · · · · · · · · · · · · · **Confession** · · · · · · · · · · · · · · · · · ·

Lord, as I look back over this list, I confess the sins of _____. Lord, please forgive me of each one, and help me to not commit these sins again. But if I do, I pray that You would convict me of that sin the very moment it's happening, so that I don't remain in that damaging conduct.

················ **Thanksgiving** ···············

Lord, I thank You that You continue to work on my heart and mind, so that I can become more like You. Lord, specifically, I thank You for helping me stay focused on You in this situation...

················ **Intercession** ···············

Lord, since _____ has been raised with Christ, set his/her heart on things above, where Christ is, seated at Your right hand. Set _____'s mind on things above, not on earthly things.

FROM COLOSSIANS 3:1-2

················ **Petition** ···············

Since I have been raised with Christ, help me continuously set my heart and mind on things above, where Christ is, seated at Your right hand. Lord, I pray that You would quickly convict me when my focus waivers.

FROM COLOSSIANS 3:1-2

20

Pride of Life

· Sally ·

*For all that is in the world, the lust of the flesh and
the lust of the eyes and the boastful pride of life, is
not from the Father, but is from the world.*

1 John 2:16

*I*n the very first book of the Bible, we see the fall of mankind and how sin enters into our world. Deception, pride, and lust are front and center.

> "You will not certainly die," the serpent said to the woman. "For God knows that when you eat from it your eyes will be opened, and you will be like God, knowing good and evil." When the woman saw that the fruit of the tree was good for food and pleasing to the eye, and also desirable for gaining wisdom, she took some and ate it. She also gave some to her husband, who was with her, and he ate it (Genesis 3:4-6 NIV).

It has been happening the same way ever since. "For all have sinned and fall short of the glory of God," Romans 3:23. Are we hopeless cases, unable to be "pure and blameless for the day of Christ" (Philippians 1:10 NIV)? No, we are never hopeless with God on our side!

111

1 Thessalonians 4:3-8

For this is the will of God, your sanctification; that is, that you abstain from sexual immorality; that each of you know how to possess his own vessel in sanctification and honor, not in lustful passion, like the Gentiles who do not know God; and that no man transgress and defraud his brother in the matter because the Lord is the avenger in all these things, just as we also told you before and solemnly warned you. For God has not called us for the purpose of impurity, but in sanctification. So, he who rejects this is not rejecting man but the God who gives His Holy Spirit to you.

God is the One who sanctifies us. He is our "Jehovah Mekoddishkem," the One who sets us apart. "You shall consecrate yourselves therefore and be holy, for I am the LORD your God. You shall keep My statutes and practice them; I am the LORD who sanctifies you" (Leviticus 20:7-8).

As God sets us apart for His glorious purposes, we have a part in the sanctification. God gives us an example through the children of Israel in the book of Joshua. God was calling His people to a land where He would empower them to fulfill their great destiny. The children of Israel had just finished wandering in a desert of grumbling, complaining, and unbelief for 40 years. Usually, when we grumble and complain it is because we want what we don't have. We aren't trusting God, and our unbelief is fueled with pride that we think we know better than the Creator of the universe.

....

We are never hopeless with God on our side.

....

After repenting of this, the Israelites went forth with courageous faith through the Jordan River during the height of flood season. And as soon as they stepped out in faith, God brought fear to the hearts of their enemies (Joshua 2:11), and led the Israelites forward into the land He had promised them. He had planned for them victory, peace, and rest, a place where they and their children could worship God and bring Him glory so all the nations would know God. Unfortunately, as we read later in the Old Testament, the temptation of pride would defeat them!

Today, let's take an honest look at the pride in our own life.

> Pride goes before destruction, and a haughty spirit before stumbling (Proverbs 16:18).

> Watch over your heart with all diligence, for from it flow the springs of life (Proverbs 4:23).

What flows out of your heart? Is it pride, complaining and unbelief?

Our God, Jehovah Mekoddishkem, hears when you confess your sins, and then His Holy Spirit will empower you to overcome any sin that stands between you and God. He can give you freedom and victory over the bondage of the sin of pride and lust, which often go hand-in-hand.

When you confess your sins, let the healing of His word empower you forward in the most amazing life you can imagine. In John 17:17-19, Jesus prays, "Sanctify them in the truth; Your word is truth. As You sent Me into the world, I also have sent them into the world. For their sakes I sanctify Myself, that they themselves also may be sanctified in truth."

Are you ready to go forth victoriously? Open up your heart to Him and He will bring healing and strength!

· **Praise** · · · · · · · · · · · · · · · · · · ·

Lord, I praise You for You are the Lord who sanctifies. Hebrews 10:10-14 says, "… we have been sanctified through the offering of the body of Jesus Christ once for all. Every priest stands daily ministering and offering time after time the same sacrifices, which can never take away sins; but He, having offered one sacrifice for sins for all time, sat down at the right hand of God, waiting from that time onward until His enemies be made a footstool for His feet. For by one offering He has perfected for all time those who are sanctified." I praise You for Your sacrifice which makes me clean before You.

Confession

Lord, search my heart and mind, and cleanse me anew. You understand every intent of each one of my thoughts. Show me which ones are prideful and impure, so I can confess them before You.

FROM 1 CHRONICLES 28:9

Thanksgiving

Thank You for Your forgiveness, that through Your promises I can walk in Your divine nature.

Intercession

Now may the God of peace Himself sanctify _____ entirely; and may his/her spirit and soul and body be preserved complete, without blame at the coming of our Lord Jesus Christ.

FROM 1 THESSALONIANS 5:23

Petition

Now may the God of peace Himself sanctify me entirely; and may my spirit and soul and body be preserved complete, without blame at the coming of our Lord Jesus Christ.

FROM 1 THESSALONIANS 5:23

Empowered Through Thanksgiving

The third step of prayer is *thanksgiving*: intentionally remembering the answers to our prayers. Sometimes, especially in the midst of hard times, being thankful can be a difficult discipline. But God calls us to "give thanks in all circumstances" (1 Thessalonians 5:18 NIV). By having a thankful heart, the Lord can empower us to lift our eyes off the obstacle in front of us and onto the only one who can remove the obstacle. In fact, that obstacle might just flourish into thanksgiving in years to come.

Rejoice always, pray continually, give thanks in all circumstances; for this is God's will for you in Christ Jesus.

1 THESSALONIANS 5:16-18 NIV

21

Giving Thanks Is a Mighty Weapon

································· Sally ·····················

We will not conceal them from their children, but tell to
the generation to come the praises of the LORD, and His
strength and His wondrous works that He has done.

PSALM 78:4

*D*id you know that thanksgiving is a mighty weapon in your armor of God? Thanksgiving activates an important part of the armor: the shield of faith. Each time you thank God for what He has done, it automatically rises up your shield of faith.

I want us to think about the shield of faith described in Ephesians 6. "In addition to all, taking up the shield of faith with which you will be able to extinguish *all* the flaming arrows of the evil one" (Ephesians 6:16, emphasis added).

God says *all*! So our shield of faith can extinguish everything the enemy is sending our way! We want that shield of faith to be large, don't we? As we begin to thank God, our faith grows, the enemy loses his foothold in our lives. Every thanksgiving helps defeat the enemy and empowers us forward.

Each year the women of Moms in Prayer International go to battle for the lives of their children, the other children of the school, the teachers, the administrators, and the other staff. At the end of the school year, many groups have a time of thanksgiving to recount what God has done in answer to their prayers. As each woman has learned to pray using God's Word, they witness Him answer powerfully! Some of the women share with me how they had lost hope until this time of remembering what God has done. As they heard all the thanksgivings, those answers to prayer, small and large for the children and schools, they knew they could go forward victoriously.

Let's look at Psalm 78:4-16 together:

> We will not conceal them from their children,
>   But tell to the generation to come
>   the praises of the LORD,
>   And His strength and His wondrous works
>   that He has done.

> For He established a testimony in Jacob
> And appointed a law in Israel,
> Which He commanded our fathers
> That they should teach them to their children,
> That the generation to come might know,
>   *even* the children *yet* to be born,
> *That* they may arise and tell *them* to their children,
> That they should put their confidence in God
> And not forget the works of God,
> But keep His commandments,
> And not be like their fathers,
> A stubborn and rebellious generation,
> A generation that did not prepare its heart
> And whose spirit was not faithful to God.

> The sons of Ephraim were archers equipped with bows,
> *Yet* they turned back in the day of battle.
> They did not keep the covenant of God
> And refused to walk in His law;
> They forgot His deeds
> And His miracles that He had shown them.
> He wrought wonders before their fathers
> In the land of Egypt, in the field of Zoan.
> He divided the sea and caused them to pass through,
> And He made the waters stand up like a heap.

Then He led them with the cloud by day
And all the night with a light of fire.
He split the rocks in the wilderness
And gave *them* abundant drink like the ocean depths.
He brought forth streams also from the rock
And caused waters to run down like rivers.

In Psalm 78 the Lord reminds His people to not forget His commands or the deeds He has done and to tell of them to their children. We saw how the sons of Ephraim were dressed and armed for battle but turned back because they had forgotten what God had done for them.

Each day, you and I have an opportunity to walk victoriously, empowered through thanksgiving, moving forward in battle with that shield of faith activated through thanksgiving. We are marching toward the goal God has called each of us toward.

In the book of Joshua, the people of Israel were led by God to miraculously cross the Jordan River, in the height of flood season, to take possession of the Promised Land. In Chapter 4, God told them to take 12 stones from the river and place them on dry land. God instructed them to tell their children what He had done for them and the stones were to be a memorial to the sons of Israel forever.

After crossing the Jordan, the children of Israel would begin to battle their enemies for the land God was going to give them. He would even fight for them, but they had to move forward with faith in Him. They could look back on these rocks and remember what God had done for them.

What Promised Land is in front of you that God wants you to take possession of? Are you praying for a wayward child who has wandered from the faith? Begin to thank God for what He has already done. Are you struggling in a marriage or with a friend or relative? Transform your thinking by focusing on what you're thankful for in that situation, and watch God bring healing.

I don't know what you are facing, but God does. As you thank Him for what He has done, your shield of faith begins to rise and your worries, problems, and fears begin to decrease.

Praise

Many, LORD my God, are the wonders you have done, the things you planned for us. None can compare with you; were I to speak and tell of your deeds, they would be too many to declare.

PSALM 40:5 NIV

Confession

Lord in the midst of the battle I want to run and not remember all You have done for me! Lord, please forgive me.

Thanksgiving

Today, Lord, I thank You for...

Intercession

Lord, help _____ remember Your deeds and Your miracles of long ago. Help him/her consider all Your works and meditate on all Your mighty deeds.

FROM PSALM 77:11-12 NIV

Petition

Lord, help me remember Your deeds and Your miracles of long ago. Help me consider all Your works and meditate on all Your mighty deeds.

FROM PSALM 77:11-12 NIV

22

Offering a Sacrifice of Thanksgiving

· · · · · · · · · · · · · · · · · Cyndie · · · · · · · · · · · · · · · ·

*"Make thankfulness your sacrifice to God, and keep the vows
you made to the Most High. Then call on me when you are
in trouble, and I will rescue you, and you will give me glory."*

PSALM 50:14-15 NLT

*G*iving thanks to the Lord is easy when a prayer is answered, when
you or your loved one gets accepted into the coveted program,
team, school, or job. When life is surprisingly good, thanksgiving
pours from our heart like a waterfall after the rain. We are filled with
joy to overflowing.

But overflowing joy is not a continuous state of being. Our emotions can ebb and flow like the waves upon the sand. When life is good
for a long period of time, sometimes we forget to give thanks to our
Lord. Instead, we expect good things to happen, for jobs to be stable,
for cars to run smoothly, for roofs not to leak.

It's also true that when life is hard—finances are tight, relationships
are frustrating, health is tenuous, kids are rebellious—thanksgiving can
be downright painful. Our thoughts can easily go to "what ifs." What
if the cancerous mass spreads? What if the surgery goes wrong? What
if I lose my job? What if my child fails out of school? What if my teen's
sullenness signifies a deeper issue? What if they're involved in destruc-
tive behaviors like cutting, drug use, or gangs?

Those "what ifs" suffocate our joy, stifle our ability to move forward,
and shackle our minds. But God's Word offers a way out. As we "set our

mind on things above and not on things that are on earth" (Colossians 3:2), we can refocus and begin to see our circumstances through God's eyes. The best way to cultivate this new vantage point is through a "sacrifice of thanksgiving" or, as Psalm 116:17 (NIV) calls it, "a thank offering" — "I will sacrifice a thank offering to you and call on the name of the LORD."

Offering thanks to the Lord is not always easy. Yet, it's a discipline that will transform not only your thinking but also your prayer life. Thanksgiving should accompany our prayer requests. Re-read Psalm 50:14-15 at the top of this devotional. Did you notice what we're supposed to do first in difficult times? We first offer our sacrifice of thanksgiving, keeping our vows to the Most High. And *then* we call on Him when we are in trouble. What is the promise? That He "will rescue you." And our response? We will give God the glory. That principle reminds me of Philippians 4:6, "Do not be anxious about anything, but in every situation, by prayer and petition, with thanksgiving, present your requests to God" (NIV). In *every* situation, we bring our concerns to God *with thanksgiving*. Even though we want to jump straight into our list of needs when we're praying, we must not ever forget to bathe our requests in thanksgiving.

When life is difficult or frustrating and answers to prayer seem to come slowly, I love to re-read this passage:

> Though the fig tree does not bud
> and there are no grapes on the vines,
> though the olive crop fails
> and the fields produce no food,
> though there are no sheep in the pen
> and no cattle in the stalls,
> yet I will rejoice in the LORD,
> I will be joyful in God my Savior.
>
> The Sovereign LORD is my strength;
> he makes my feet like the feet of a deer,
> he enables me to tread on the heights
> (Habakkuk 3:17-19 NIV).

Even when, from the world's perspective, thanksgiving might come slowly, we can still determine to be thankful, to be "joyful in God my Savior."

How is your heart? Are you feeling thankful and joyful? Or are you feeling overwhelmed and frustrated? Spend time giving God an offering of thanksgiving.

• • • • • • • • • • • • • • • • • Praise • • • • • • • • • • • • • • • • • •

Oh Lord, I praise You that You are our rescuer. As Psalm 50:15 says, "Then call on me when you are in trouble, and I will rescue you" (NLT). How I praise You for that promise, that You are assuredly my rescuer.

• • • • • • • • • • • • • • • • Confession • • • • • • • • • • • • • • • •

Lord, forgive me for the times that I forget to offer a sacrifice of thanksgiving. Please alert me daily as soon as I begin to move my eyes off You and begin to feel ungrateful, so that I can confess immediately. Help me have a soft heart to hear Your correction.

• • • • • • • • • • • • • • Thanksgiving • • • • • • • • • • • • • • •

Lord, here is my offering of thanksgiving. Even though it might be difficult, I thank You for...

•••••••••••••••• Intercession ••••••••••••••••

Lord, help _____ make thankfulness a sacrifice
to You and to keep the vows made to You, Most
High. Help _____ call on You in times of trouble
and rescue him/her, so he/she will give You glory.

FROM PSALM 50:14-15

•••••••••••••••• Petition ••••••••••••••••

Lord, I pray that for myself, as well. Help me always
make thankfulness a sacrifice to You and to keep my vows
to You, the Most High. Help me remember to do that
first before I call on You when I am in trouble, knowing
that You will rescue me and I will give You glory.

FROM PSALM 50:14-15

23

Remembering Our Thanksgivings

················ Sally ···················

But as for me, the nearness of God is my good;
I have made the Lord God my refuge,
That I may tell of all Your works.

PSALM 73:28

My husband takes pictures as we travel. He's able to capture some of the most beautiful places. Each photograph tells a story of an incredible moment, scene, or adventure. Every so often we look through them and remember where God has taken us. We especially enjoy the images of nature. They help us to notice and appreciate the beauty of God's creation. Time and again, we witness evidence of the care He takes for all of it: from the smallest plant that receives rain and sun so it may grow, to the largest sea creature.

When you and I look at creation we see and know what God has done. We also see a picture of who He is. His action in creation paints a picture of awesomeness, beauty, power, sovereignty, and detailed attention.

Matthew 6:26-30

Look at the birds of the air, that they do not sow nor reap nor gather into barns and yet your heavenly Father feeds them. Are you not worth more than they? And who of you by being worried can add a single hour to his

life? And why are you worried about clothing? Observe
how the lilies of the field grow; they do not toil nor do
they spin, yet I say to you that not even Solomon in all
his glory clothed himself like one of these. But if God
so clothes the grass of the field which is alive today and
tomorrow is thrown into the furnace will He not much
more clothe you?

Do you ever thank God for His creation? Do you ever stand in awe
of all He has done for you? Do you ponder the work of God in a tree
and thank Him for the oxygen it brings so we can breathe, or how it
shows us the seasons of life. Do you rejoice in how God delivers fruit
to eat and shade from the sun through His gift of trees? All this, God
has provided for you and me!

Then there are heart pictures of the places God has taken us. These
don't always seem so beautiful at the time we are experiencing them.
My friend Nancy and I have been praying together for our families for
decades now. One afternoon before we began to pray she brought out
some journals that had our prayers in them. She began to read them.
First, we were astonished at all the trouble that had come our way and
then we were thankful. Oh, how God had cared for us through it all.
So many amazing answers to our prayers in the hard places our families had been. God answered above all we could have ever expected.
Have you thanked God lately for taking you from dark places to Himself and His light?

One of my friends at Bible study class knew I prayed for children
and schools, so she would give me prayer requests for her son. I told
her I would pray but invited her to come to our Moms in Prayer group
and pray with us for her son. This went on for about 10 years before
she finally came. That very first week, during our time of thanksgiving,
she cried with tears of joy thanking God for this place. She was finally
in God's throne with sisters surrounding her and praying with her for
her son.

Do you thank God that you can boldly and confidently enter His
throne room of grace to find mercy and help in your time of need

(Hebrews 4:16)? Or that you have brothers and sisters who will carry the burden with you to God? It is God who gave us prayer, access to the most intimate relationship with the only one who can answer our prayers. There is so much to be thankful for.

Another picture is the one I consider to be a faith-family portrait. I get to see what God is doing around the world as God's daughters gather to pray! How He is gathering women together in over 140 countries worldwide. He is unifying hearts, cultures, languages and denominations in Christ through prayer. While visiting France, I saw a Catholic mom, a Mennonite mom, and a Charismatic mom all unified in prayer. They were one in prayer and in Christ.

As I read reports from women in our groups, my heart fills with thanksgiving for what He is doing as they pray. God is enlarging the hearts of the women to pray for all the children in their schools. In Moms in Prayer International our vision is that every school and every child in the world will be covered with prayer.

In several countries of Southern Africa, the AIDs epidemic has left many children without parents to care for them or pray for them. Child-headed households are very common in these countries. My joy of thanksgiving soared when I heard about a Moms in Prayer group in Zambia who adopted a "child-headed" household to cover each of those children in prayer.

In your heart, capture pictures of the truths of God as you thank Him that:

- You have been given great precious promises by God. 2 Peter 1:4
- Your needs are met by God. Philippians 4:19
- You have been made complete in Christ. Colossians 2:10
- Nothing can separate you from the love of God. Romans 8:35

We can take and celebrate pictures of our lives with hearts of thanksgiving when we remember all that God has done for us and for those we lift up in prayer.

· · · · · · · · · · · · · · · · · · Praise · · · · · · · · · · · · · · · · · · ·

Lord, I praise You for You are a good God who withholds no good thing. Therefore, I can trust You and wait on Your perfect timing.

FROM PSALM 52:9 AND PSALM 84:11

· · · · · · · · · · · · · · · · Confession · · · · · · · · · · · · · · · · · ·

Lord I ask forgiveness for not thanking You lately for all You have done for me. Please forgive me.

· · · · · · · · · · · · · · · Thanksgiving · · · · · · · · · · · · · · · · ·

I give You thanks for...

· · · · · · · · · · · · · · · · Intercession · · · · · · · · · · · · · · · · ·

Lord, help _____ know that the nearness of God is his/her good. Help _____ make You his/her refuge, that _____ may tell of all Your works.

FROM PSALM 73:28

· · · · · · · · · · · · · · · · Petition · · · · · · · · · · · · · · · · · ·

But as for me, the nearness of God is my good;
I have made the Lord GOD my refuge,
That I may tell of all Your works.

PSALM 73:28

24

Can We Really Give Thanks in All Circumstances?

· · · · · · · · · · · · · · · · · · Cyndie · · · · · · · · · · · · · · · · · · ·

*Rejoice always, pray continually, give thanks in all
circumstances; for this is God's will for you in Christ Jesus.*

1 THESSALONIANS 5:16-18

*I*n less than 20 words, we can feel convicted by this verse in First Thessalonians. "Always." "Continually." "In all circumstances." Yikes!
Do we rejoice *always*?

Do we pray continually? *Continually*? Yes, that's what it says. Other versions say, "Pray without ceasing"; "Pray constantly"; "never stop praying." The Amplified version goes one step further and explains, "be unceasing and persistent in prayer."

And what about verse 18? "Give thanks in all circumstances; for this is God's will for you in Christ Jesus." Umm, did you catch that? It's God's will for you and me to give thanks, not just in the easy stuff, but in ALL circumstances. That one little three-letter word includes health problems, job layoffs, relationship struggles, financial woes, and any other kind of frustrating, stressful circumstances. God's will for us is to be thankful.

In fact, the mere act of being thankful can transform a grumpy heart into a joyful one. Specifically, when we start thanking God for our blessings and answered prayers, we are reminded that we serve a big God who loves us and cares about us. Even during times of frustration, agony, pain, or sorrow, having a thankful heart can help our trials feel more bearable and less overpowering.

But be careful of saving the thanksgiving principle for just the big doozy of a trial. Remember, "in all circumstances" even includes the little annoyances that happen every day.

I like to share this simple illustration about the importance of being thankful. One Saturday morning, I woke up excited to make an omelet doused in salsa verde. (Strange, yes. But very tasty.) Unfortunately, I was out of the delicious green salsa. So I begrudgingly made a blander-than-desired breakfast and went to the grocery store to fill up our fridge.

Of course, one of the first items in my shopping cart was salsa verde! Mmm, my new plan was a quesadilla doused in the green goodness for lunch. Since grumpiness typically festers and grows, my shopping trip became overwhelmed with the dark cloud of crabbiness. Most of my regular items were unavailable, and I had to purchase alternatives—like a glass bottle of salsa verde instead of plastic. I plodded through the shopping trip, grumbling to myself that it was a much longer, more frustrating, and more expensive trip than planned. As I began bringing the groceries into the house, one item didn't quite make it. I lifted up the paper bag from the car and something went crashing to the ground. Yep, the salsa verde in the glass jar. Sometimes it's the weirdest things that set us off. And this was it. If I was a cartoon, steam would have been spewing out of my ears. Suddenly everything was maddening. Grocery shopping was frustrating. Putting the groceries away by myself after I just spent forever purchasing them was annoying! Being a mother was hard! Life was difficult!

But, thankfully, the Holy Spirit's gentle reminder cut through my crabbiness: I had not had my quiet time yet. I put away the cold items, then plopped down in my chair, and the Holy Spirit convicted me of my ungrateful attitude. So I started thanking God...for my house, for the refrigerator that was old but kept the food cold, for the car that got me to and from the grocery store, for the (somewhat limited) funds that allowed me to even buy groceries (and to splurge a couple extra dollars on good salsa), for my family, for God's Word.

Then I lifted up my eyes. What did I see out my window? Trees! Beautiful trees outlining a lovely blue sky. I took a deep breath and thanked God for His creativity in designing so many variations of green, and for allowing me to see them beyond the brick fence in my backyard. In that instant, my heart changed. My circumstances had not changed—only my attitude. But changing our attitude changes everything!

· · · · · · · · · · · · · · · · · Praise · · · · · · · · · · · · · · · ·

Heavenly Father, we praise You that You not only tell us to be thankful in all circumstances, but You help us to do so.

· · · · · · · · · · · · · · · Confession · · · · · · · · · · · · · · · ·

Please forgive me for the times that I am not thankful or rejoicing or praying. You want to have a continuous, consistent relationship with me, yet I often get so distracted by the concerns of life. Forgive me for that, Lord, and help me remember that being thankful helps me keep my eyes on You.

· · · · · · · · · · · · · · Thanksgiving · · · · · · · · · · · · · ·

Lord, as I thank You in ALL circumstances, I want to specifically thank You for...

· · · · · · · · · · · · · · · · · Intercession · · · · · · · · · · · · · · · · ·

Help _____ rejoice always, pray continually, give thanks in all circumstances; for this is Your will for him/her in Christ Jesus.

From 1 Thessalonians 5 niv

· · · · · · · · · · · · · · · · · Petition ·

Help me rejoice always, pray continually, give thanks in all circumstances; for this is Your will for me in Christ Jesus.

From 1 Thessalonians 5 niv

25

Thanking God for His Discipline

· · · · · · · · · · · · · · · · · · · Sally · · · · · · · · · · · · · · · · · ·

And have you completely forgotten this word of
encouragement that addresses you as a father addresses
his son? It says, "My son, do not make light of the
Lord's discipline, and do not lose heart when he
rebukes you, because the Lord disciplines the one he
loves, and he chastens everyone he accepts as his son."

HEBREWS 12:5-6 NIV

I remember watching a man drive the wrong way down a one way
street, to the horror of others. Horns honking at him did not deter
him. Only a police car pulling him over and giving him a ticket for
going the wrong way stopped him from hurting himself and others.

I think of the gentle rebuke Jesus gave Martha in Luke 10:41-43:
"Martha, Martha", the Lord answered, "you are worried and upset
about many things, but few things are needed—or indeed only one.
Mary has chosen what is better, and it will not be taken away from
her" (NIV). Martha learned and grew into the woman God intended
her to be.

Middle school can be a challenging time for children. They want
to fit into the norm or with their peers. They don't even realize they are
being conformed to this world instead of being transformed by God to
demonstrate His good and acceptable will (from Romans 12:2). So in
my Moms in Prayer group we began to pray that our children would
be caught each time they did something they shouldn't, even a small

offense. One afternoon during our prayer time while we were thanking God, all three of us moms thanked God that our kids were caught doing what they should not be doing!

Now you may wonder why we would thank Him for this. Shouldn't we be mad and horrified? Sometimes we are, but we understand that God so loves our children that He does not want them to stay in their sin, but be overcomers that impact our world for Christ. He wants them to let go of everything that hinders them from His great calling on their lives. I remember one mom who thanked God that her son stopped even trying to get away with anything, because he knew he would only get caught and disciplined.

I know moms who prayed that their children would be caught by the police so they would not be killed by drug dealers...and it was in jail that their children found Jesus! As hard as it is to thank God in the tough circumstances, you and I can know that God is working in them. We can trust Him.

Women in prison have told me that they were very thankful they were caught so they could surrender their lives to Jesus. Jesus is now empowering them to live a victorious life. From prison, they are now impacting other prisoners and their families for Christ.

We all can be in a personal prison if we don't see God's discipline as something to be thankful for. Oh how I want to have the peaceful fruit of righteousness and to share in His holiness, so I will learn to be thankful even when it is hard because God loves me!

Hebrews 12:11

All discipline for the moment seems not to be joyful, but sorrowful; yet to those who have been trained by it, afterwards it yields the peaceful fruit of righteousness.

How about you? Are you thankful when God disciplines you? If He did not love you He would not discipline you. If God did not see great things for your life, He would leave you just as you are going the wrong way. But thankfully, "He who began a good work in you will perfect it" (Philippians 1:6). As God disciplines us, He is preparing us to be empowered for every good work.

2 Timothy 2:19-21

Nevertheless, the firm foundation of God stands, having this seal, "The Lord knows those who are His," and, "Everyone who names the name of the Lord is to abstain from wickedness." Now in a large house there are not only gold and silver vessels, but also vessels of wood and of earthenware, and some to honor and some to dishonor. Therefore, if anyone cleanses himself from these things, he will be a vessel for honor, sanctified, useful to the Master, prepared for every good work.

Let us thank God for His discipline so we can be vessels empowered and ready for every good work!

· · · · · · · · · · · · · · · · · · **Praise** · · · · · · · · · · · · · · · · · ·

*Lord, I praise You that You love me enough to discipline
me. And You discipline me because I am Yours and You
are mine. And I praise You that You who began a good
work in me will complete it until the day of Christ.*

FROM PHILLIPIANS 1:6

· · · · · · · · · · · · · · · · · **Confession** · · · · · · · · · · · · · · · · ·

*Lord, I confess to You the times that I do not heed Your
discipline and go the wrong direction bringing harm
to myself and others. Please forgive me for...*

······················· **Thanksgiving** ·······················

Thank You that Your discipline brings the peaceful fruit of righteousness to those who are trained by it and that I can share in Your holiness. And thank You that You disciplined me for...

······················· **Intercession** ·······················

I pray _____ will not make light of the Lord's discipline and not lose heart when rebuked, because You, Lord, discipline the ones You love, and chasten everyone You accept as Your child.

FROM HEBREWS 12:5-6

······················· **Petition** ·······················

Lord, empower me to be Your vessel that is wholly dedicated and beneficial to You for every good work.

FROM 2 TIMOTHY 2:19-21

26

When Tears Turn to Cheers

· · · · · · · · · · · · · · · · · Cyndie · · · · · · · · · · · · · · · · · ·

The LORD has done great things for us,
and we are filled with joy.

PSALM 126:3 NIV

A couple days after my second child was born, I stumbled upon
Psalm 126:3 during my quiet time. As I read that verse, my heart
leapt with delight. My family of four was complete, and I was truly
"filled with joy" because "the LORD has done great things for us." I
highlighted that verse on my elated *"She's here!"* email broadcast, on
the printed announcement, and it's even featured on a picture frame
in our home.

With the birth of any child comes much rejoicing. But often the
more adversity one experiences, the sweeter the thanksgiving. When
fears and tears turn to prayers and then cheers, the result is much
rejoicing.

Some pregnancies are what the doctor might call "text book." Others, however, are marked with bumps along the road, and, yes, so much
bigger than any one "baby bump." And, while I know plenty of people who have worse pregnancy stories, my second pregnancy had its
share of uncertainties. For starters, I think my baby knew how much
I love Christmas, because she thought that would be an ideal time to
try to make her way into the world despite the fact she wasn't due until
late March. I distinctly remember the day I went to lay down on the
couch in the women's restroom at work. The contractions were too

consistent for Braxton Hicks. "Will my baby be born in a newsroom?" I wondered between deep breaths and much prayer. But God was gracious. With the help of medication, my sweet baby stayed nestled in my womb for a few more weeks, while I was put on disability.

Then there was the series of standard tests, which I had a propensity to fail, one after the other, including the one for gestational diabetes. I thought I had fulfilled all quotas for pregnancy problems. But, alas, my asthma kicked up into full gear, spurred on by a ruckus bout of bronchitis. I stuffed all the inhalers and medications into a large baggie and declared to my OBGYN, "This can't possibly be good for my baby!" But the doctor insisted that lack of oxygen would be far worse than any of the mild side effects. I sighed (a rather wheezy sigh) and dutifully continued taking the cornucopia of asthma and bronchitis medications.

Thankfully, my baby held on until 22 days before her due date. Then, in a whirl of alarms and warning lights, and the doctor's valiant effort to avoid a caesarean section, she arrived. Long and skinny, a pinker—and, surprisingly, healthier—version of her bronzed brother. The next morning, when the extremely loud pediatrician arrived in our room before the sun even hinted it was a new day, he declared—quite boisterously—that the only visible sign she was not officially full-term was that she didn't have wrinkles on her feet. While my son had to be re-admitted for jaundice as a newborn, this little pink bundle was able to come home and stay. And we were all delighted, especially her big brother.

I have so often quoted Psalm 126:3, that I had almost forgotten its context. Sometimes it gives a fresh perspective to read a Bible passage in a different version. Here is Psalm 126 in the New Living Translation:

A song for pilgrims ascending to Jerusalem.

When the LORD brought back his exiles to Jerusalem,
it was like a dream!
We were filled with laughter,
and we sang for joy.

And the other nations said,
"What amazing things the LORD has done for them."
Yes, the LORD has done amazing things for us!
What joy!

Restore our fortunes, LORD,
as streams renew the desert.
Those who plant in tears
will harvest with shouts of joy.
They weep as they go to plant their seed,
but they sing as they return with the harvest.

Oftentimes, when life is running along without any major bumps in the road, we can forget to be thankful. But when we have to endure an uphill climb first, we develop a greater appreciate for the destination. Blessings are always sweeter after a long, bumpy journey. As Proverbs 13:12 says, "Hope deferred makes the heart sick, but a longing fulfilled is a tree of life" (NIV).

Re-read Psalm 126:5: "Those who plant in tears will harvest with shouts of joy" (NLT). What are you planting with tears? Are you a young parent with toddlers? Or are you trying to set up boundaries for your teenagers? Are you in a struggling marriage? Is work so dreary that your Monday morning blues last all week? Or maybe you're a homeschool parent frustrated with teaching unmotivated children. Be encouraged by verse 6, "They weep as they go to plant their seed, but they sing as they return with the harvest."

When thanksgivings are hard to find, look toward the joy that is to come. Be thankful that God is working it all together for a good purpose (Romans 8:28). Even though you might not be able to see the joy awaiting you on the other side, be thankful that your season of planting in tears can result in a harvest of great joy.

Praise

Oh, how I praise You that You are a God of joy. You desire to shower me with blessings that come in Your perfect timing, and I so praise You for that.

Confession

Lord, forgive me for the times that I take my eyes off You and forget that You are working out a bigger plan, that the joy planted through sorrow will be even more fruitful.

Thanksgiving

Lord, I thank You for the desert times when I have experienced Your refreshing streams which renew my parched heart. Thank You, specifically, for turning my sorrow to joy during...

Intercession

Restore _____'s fortunes, Lord, as streams renew the desert. As he/she plants in tears, help _____ harvest with shouts of joy.

From Psalm 126:4-5

Petition

Restore my fortunes Lord, as streams renew the desert. As I plant in tears, help me harvest with shouts of joy.

From Psalm 126:4-5

27

Thanksgiving: A Holy Spirit Party

· · · · · · · · · · · · · · · · · · Sally · · · · · · · · · · · · · · · · · ·

Rejoice in the Lord always. I will say it again:
Rejoice! Let your gentleness be evident to all. The Lord is near.

PHILIPPIANS 4:4-5 NIV

*I*f you were to ask me what thanksgiving is, I would tell you it is a Holy Spirit party rejoicing in answered prayer, thanking God for what He has done. Now you may be thinking: How can we rejoice always, when life can be so very hard? We live in a fallen world with fallen humans and many perils and problems. Yet, we can rejoice as we come to God with a thankful heart.

One of my dearest friends died of breast cancer over 23 years ago. She left behind her three precious young girls and a grieving husband who loved her dearly. But she also left a powerful legacy of prayer and a grateful heart in the midst of a terrible trial.

I met my friend in Moms in Prayer where we prayed for our children and schools. We were strangers, but once we prayed together our hearts were blended together. After that first time, she came over to my house uninvited with a cup of coffee and a gift of fellowship. She would become my mentor, and I would be on a journey watching someone live out James 1:2, counting it "all joy" when she met trials of various kinds.

....

We can rejoice as we come to
God with a thankful heart.

....

She grew up in a Christian home with a dad who was a pastor, and she had walked with the Lord for many years. I was new in my faith and had much to learn. I watched intently as she was called to walk through the valley of the shadow of death. And I was there for her if she needed anything.

Cancer can be a cruel task master and also a place where Christ can become the center of your life. "Your life is hidden with Christ in God. When Christ who is our life, is revealed, then you also will be revealed with Him in glory" (Colossians 3:3-4). For my friend, it would be a place where Christ became the center of her life and through her He would be glorified.

We had a choice: We could look at this situation horrified, hopeless, angry, and defeated, or we could begin to thank God for the big and little things. We chose to thank Him each day. Even though she faced all that cancer brought—she faced fear, unknowns, chemo, hair loss, and all the "whys"—yet, there were times when we laughed until it hurt. There would be days filled with both tears of loss and joys of thanksgiving.

One day I went to pick up her kids. Her mom came out in tears and expressed how she did not and could not understand how her daughter, my friend, could spend time praising and thanking God. I did not blame her mom for her pain; instead, I shared about some of the blessings her daughter and I were thankful for. Her mom was moved from tears to a smile with a grateful heart.

One night around midnight my friend called me so we could pray together. She said she knew God could still heal her if He wanted, but she felt He was bringing her home to heaven. So we began to pray for her husband's next wife and the stepmom for her children. She prayed the most beautiful prayer for this woman who would become her children's new mother and her husband's new wife. And God answered all her requests—except her request that their new mom would not have thinner thighs than her! She kept her joy until the end, and oh how God answered her prayers for her family.

As I went through this journey with my dear friend and we said goodbye until we see each other again in heaven, I learned by her example to have a thankful heart. Her thankful heart empowered her to live her life out to the very end, bringing God glory and joy to herself and those around her.

After her death when I would miss her or hurt for her precious daughters, I would start thanking God for what He did during and after her death:

- The town raised enough money for blood transfusions that kept her alive a little longer so her family could have those precious times with her.

- Her kids had rides to school when she was too sick to take them.

- She looked good in a wig.

- She could still stand up, leaning against me in church to worship God.

- He gave us all the years we had with her. Even though the time was short, it was a gift.

- Several came to know the Lord through her life and death.

- God is still answering the prayers she prayed for her family over 20 years ago.

- All three of her girls are thriving!

- God walked with all who went through this journey with her.

- She is safely home with our heavenly Father.

Thankful hearts empower us beyond the pain and suffering, to find joy no matter what!

· · · · · · · · · · · · Praise · · · · · · · · · · · ·

Lord, I praise You that You empower me to be strong and courageous. I need not be afraid or discouraged because You, Lord my God, will be with me wherever I go. Even if it is in the valley of the shadow of death I fear no evil for You are with me. Your rod and Your staff comfort me!

FROM JOSHUA 1:9 AND PSALM 23

· · · · · · · · · · · · Confession · · · · · · · · · · ·

I ask for forgiveness when I do not rejoice because I have forgotten the goodness of the Lord in the land of the living.

FROM PSALM 27:13

· · · · · · · · · · · · Thanksgiving · · · · · · · · · ·

Thank You, Lord, that You stay with us and promise to never leave us nor forsake us. In the midst of our darkest times, You carry us in Your everlasting arms.

· · · · · · · · · · · · Intercession · · · · · · · · · ·

Help _____ rejoice in You always, Lord. Help his/ her gentleness be evident to all. The Lord is near.

FROM PHILIPPIANS 4:4-5 NIV

· · · · · · · · · · · · Petition · · · · · · · · · ·

Help me, Lord, to rejoice always because my life is hidden with Christ in You. May I always have a grateful heart defeating fear and discouragement.

28

Thanksgiving Brings Light to the Darkest Days

· Cyndie ·

I cried out to God for help;
I cried out to God to hear me.
When I was in distress, I sought the Lord;
at night I stretched out untiring hands,
and I would not be comforted...
"Has God forgotten to be merciful?
Has he in anger withheld his compassion?"

Then I thought, "To this I will appeal:
the years when the Most High stretched out his right hand.
I will remember the deeds of the LORD;
yes, I will remember your miracles of long ago.
I will consider all your works
and meditate on all your mighty deeds."

Your ways, God, are holy.
What god is as great as our God?
You are the God who performs miracles;
you display your power among the peoples.

With your mighty arm you redeemed your people,
the descendants of Jacob and Joseph.

The waters saw you, God,
the waters saw you and writhed;
the very depths were convulsed.
The clouds poured down water,
the heavens resounded with thunder;

> *your arrows flashed back and forth.*
> *Your thunder was heard in the whirlwind,*
> *your lightning lit up the world;*
> *the earth trembled and quaked.*

PSALM 77:1-2, 9-18 NIV

When your heart aches, read Psalm 77. When you are in a season of waiting and wondering, read Psalm 77. When you question what God is up to, read Psalm 77.

In our book, *Unshaken*, I share about my brother-in-law Dickson and the miracle of his perfect-match kidney. Yet, before the book was officially released, I received the call that Dickson was being admitted to the intensive care unit. We begged God to heal him. And He did. Just not as we would have chosen. On February 9, 2017, Dickson met his heavenly Father face to face. Our lives suddenly felt like the storm in verses 17 and 18. Emotions of thunder and lightning shook our world. We were swept up in a whirlwind of disbelief and horror. Our world trembled and quaked.

As people began to hear of Dickson's death, stories of his life of faith poured forth from many corners of the world. One young man told my sister how he had met Dickson on an airplane and explained how encouraging Dickson had been to him. As only God can do, Dickson continued to encourage those of us who were grieving, even after his passing. Just days after becoming a widow, my sister, Cathy, stumbled upon Dickson's personal thoughts from his last Bible Study Fellowship lesson. His profound insight became the front of his memorial celebration card.

> Jesus WILL return and I can bank on that 100 percent. Jesus never makes a promise and doesn't keep it. He is preparing a place for us and will return to get us. My heart is troubled no more even with all the gloomy health issues that lie ahead of me. Whether I live or die,

I have gained heaven. I can comfort those who are in my
position and give them hope. If one has Jesus that is all
they need. —Dickson Chan, February 2, 2017

Through it all, my sister has kept her eyes on the Lord. Despite out-
rageous bills and the necessity of selling her beautiful home, she has
remained faithful to the Lord and thankful. Yes, thankful. By keeping
her eyes on the Lord and inviting friends and family to join her in lifting up specific prayer requests, she's been able to see God's provision
and love and strength repeatedly.

While we were still reeling from the shock and beginning to plan
the memorial, she wrote on her Facebook page:

> Hi everyone, I really just want to say that God is big,
> and we can trust Him. I am standing in amazement as
> I watch God take care of big and small things and even
> answering the silent concerns of my heart. I am thank-
> ful because many times we walk through trials and we
> don't see God's hand so clearly, He is showing himself
> each day. Many times a day. My heart rejoices.

A few months later, after she sold her home, moved in with her
mother-in-law and began taking care of our mom, who was having
severe heart issues, she posted this:

> Lord, God of all creation, thank You for going before
> me this week and for promising strength and wisdom.
> Thank You for knowing the plans You have in store for
> me and for those I love. Thank You, dear heavenly Father,
> I know Your heart is a good heart and Your ways always
> lead me to maturing and the building of holiness in my
> character. I don't always like the way You answer my
> prayers or the paths You take me down or the dark roads
> that are part of my journey. I do however love that I can
> trust You, at every level of trust, to be leading me down
> the BEST path and that if You say "No" to my prayer, it

is because Your ways are higher than my ways and Your
thoughts are higher than my thoughts.

Moving from a sprawling home with an amazing pool and expan-
sive view, into a room in her mother-in-law's house was not her plan.
But that was God's plan. And as we prayed for the house to sell quickly
and to just the right person, God provided: A widower with three kids
now enjoy the home where Dickson and Cathy raised their four boys.

In the midst of frustrations and unknowns, Psalm 77 echoes our
hearts and exposes the feelings of exasperation that come as we cry out
to God to answer requests that are only in His power to do so. This
psalm reminds us that we are free to share with God all of our emotions—after all, He already knows them.

But my favorite part of the psalm is that after the frustration and
questioning, the psalmist moves his eyes from the problem onto the
Problem Solver. "I recall all you have done, O LORD; I remember your
wonderful deeds of long ago. They are constantly in my thoughts. I
cannot stop thinking about your mighty works" (v. 11-12 NLT). The
psalmist intentionally stops questioning and complaining, and refo-
cuses on giving thanks to the Lord, on remembering what God has
done in the past to remind us what God is capable of in the future.

When you are in distress, when life feels like it's crumbling around
you, when the ache from your heart keeps your mind awake at night
and knots up your stomach, spend time remembering what God has
done for you. What are some specific blessings you can thank Him for?
If you need to look back in your family history or expand out to your
friends, go for it. The Psalmist did. The point is to remind ourselves
that whatever you're facing: God's got it!

Was there a time in your life where it looked like chaos was having
a party, but God came in and saved the day in a big, miraculous way?
Maybe it wasn't in your own life, but someone else's. Reflect on that
thanksgiving, and remember: He's more than capable, more than willing. He's just waiting for the ultimate perfect timing.

Are you struggling? God understands. Tell Him your feelings. Ask
His help in transforming and empowering your heart and mind to be

thankful and unshaken. When fear grips your heart, remember what God has done in the past and thank Him. Let His peace wash over you as you begin to stand firm on the path He has set out for you.

Praise

"You are the God of great wonders! You demonstrate your awesome power among the nations" (Psalm 77:14 NLT). Lord, I praise You for demonstrating Your power both throughout history as well as in my own life.

Confession

Please forgive me for the times I forget Your awesome power and forget that You are taking me through a particular path on purpose. As Psalm 77:19 so beautifully depicts, even when all I see is the mighty water, You are there guiding me through each storm of life.

Thanksgiving

Oh, how I thank You for leading me along the path You've set before me and my loved ones. As I look back over my life, I can see Your hand guiding me. Thank You for leading me through this specific stressful situation in my past...

• • • • • • • • • • • • • • • • • Intercession • • • • • • • • • • • • • • • • •

Lord, help _____ see that Your path may lead through the sea, Your way through the mighty waters, even though he/she can't see Your footprints. Lead _____ along the road You have for him/her, like a sheep following its shepherd.

FROM PSALM 77:19-20

• • • • • • • • • • • • • • • • • Petition • • • • • • • • • • • • • • • • •

Lord, help me remember that Your path may lead through the sea, Your way through the mighty waters, even though I can't see Your footprints. Lead me along the road You have for me, like a sheep following my shepherd.

FROM PSALM 77:19-20

29

We Are Triumphant in Christ!

· Sally ·

*But thanks be to God, who always leads us in triumph
in Christ, and manifests through us the sweet aroma
of the knowledge of Him in every place. For we are
a fragrance of Christ to God among those who are
being saved and among those who are perishing.*

2 Corinthians 2:14-15

How thankful I am that God leads us in victory over our sins. He leads triumphantly in Christ, victoriously, each step forward. I am thankful that Jesus conquered both the penalty of sin and the bondage of sin. God opened my eyes and turned me from darkness to light from the power of Satan to God so I could be forgiven of my sins and have a place among those who are sanctified. I am set free to be His child and am no longer captive to this world or sin. And so are you once Jesus becomes your Savior. The penalty of sin is death but the gift of God in Jesus is eternal life. Let's thank God for this immeasurable gift!

Now each of our lives can be a sweet aroma (an example of Christ's love, kindness, grace, etc.) to those around us. The picture the apostle Paul gives in 2 Corinthians 2:14-15 is a victory march. After the Romans would conquer their enemies, the soldiers would parade victoriously throughout the city sending the sweet fragrance of incense throughout the town and lifting up songs of victory while the defeated enemy was made to follow behind. The whole city would know that the Romans had been victorious.

Today this is a picture of Christians who are living empowered by Christ, who defeated the enemy when he died on the cross and rose again! As we live victoriously, we are sending a sweet aroma of Christ throughout the world. We walk in triumphant victory because of Christ's death and resurrection!

1 Corinthians 15:54-58

"Death is swallowed up in victory. O death, where is your victory? O death, where is your sting?" The sting of death is sin, and the power of sin is the law; but thanks be to God, who gives us the victory through our Lord Jesus Christ.

Therefore, my beloved brethren, be steadfast, immovable, always abounding in the work of the Lord, knowing that your toil is not in vain in the Lord.

I am empowered by Christ to walk victoriously! His gift of His Word helps us to walk in a way that is pleasing to God and brings glory to God. I am so thankful that God reveals Himself to us. This knowledge of who God is will be a sweet aroma of Christ within our own hearts. It is through knowledge of our God that we will be made steadfast and immovable. Have you thanked Him today for revealing Himself to you through His Word?

I want you to imagine the two aromas that filled the house one night in Luke 7. One was the aroma of a thankful heart, the other the smell of self-righteousness and death.

Now one of the Pharisees was requesting Him to dine with him (Jesus), and He entered the Pharisee's house and reclined at the table. And there was a woman in the city who was a sinner; and when she learned that He was reclining at the table in the Pharisee's house, she brought an alabaster vial of perfume, and standing behind Him at His feet, weeping, she began to wet His feet with her tears, and kept wiping them with the hair of her head, and kissing His feet and anointing them with the perfume. Now when the Pharisee who had invited Him saw this, he said to himself, "If this man were a prophet He would know who and what sort of person this woman is who is touching Him, that she is a sinner."

And Jesus answered him, "Simon, I have something to say to you." And he replied, "Say it, Teacher." "A money-lender had two debtors: one owed five hundred denarii, and the other fifty. When they were unable to repay, he graciously forgave them both. So which of them will love him more?" Simon answered and said, "I suppose the one whom he forgave more." And He said to him, "You have judged correctly." Turning toward the woman, He said to Simon, "Do you see this woman? I entered your house; you gave Me no water for My feet, but she has wet My feet with her tears and wiped them with her hair. You gave Me no kiss; but she, since the time I came in, has not ceased to kiss My feet. You did not anoint My head with oil, but she anointed My feet with perfume. For this reason I say to you, her sins, which are many, have been forgiven, for she loved much; but he who is forgiven little, loves little." Then He said to her, "Your sins have been forgiven" (Luke 7:36-48).

I would say this scripture describes what this woman had done. Psalm 54:6 says,
"Willingly I will sacrifice to You; I will give thanks to Your name, O LORD, for it is good."

•••••••••••••••••••••••••••••

It is through knowledge of our God that we
will be made steadfast and immovable.

•••••••••••••••••••••••••••••

With a heart of thanksgiving for your salvation, may it be a sweet aroma to God. And with a thankful heart that He leads you in triumph in Christ, may you go forward empowered to share Christ in the sweetest aroma possible.

••••••••••••••••••••• Praise •••••••••••••••••••••

*Through Him then, let us continually offer up a sacrifice
of praise to God, that is, the fruit of lips that give thanks
to His name. Lord, I praise You for You will lead me
victoriously. You enable me to be steadfast and immovable.*

Hebrews 13:15

••••••••••••••••••••• Confession •••••••••••••••••••••

*Lord I ask forgiveness for when I don't allow You to manifest a
sweet aroma through me because I am entangled with self, anger,
or other sin. Reveal to me what sin is hindering my sweet aroma.*

••••••••••••••••••••• Thanksgiving •••••••••••••••••••••

*Thank You Lord that You saved me by the gift of Your
Son and now You empower me to be Your sweet aroma
to all around me as I walk triumphant in Christ.*

· · · · · · · · · · · · · · · · Intercession · · · · · · · · · · · · · · · ·

Lord, help _____ stand in Christ so You can lead him/her in triumph. Lord, manifest in _____ the sweet aroma of the knowledge of You in every place.

FROM 2 CORINTHIANS 2:14

· · · · · · · · · · · · · · · · Petition · · · · · · · · · · · · · · · · · ·

Lord may I stand in Christ so You can lead me in triumph, and Lord, manifest in me the sweet aroma of the knowledge of You in every place.

FROM 2 CORINTHIANS 2:14

30

Thanking God for Pulling Us from the Mud and Mire

. . . . Cyndie . . . .

I waited patiently for the LORD;
he turned to me and heard my cry.
He lifted me out of the slimy pit,
out of the mud and mire;
he set my feet on a rock
and gave me a firm place to stand.
He put a new song in my mouth,
a hymn of praise to our God.
Many will see and fear the LORD
and put their trust in him.

Blessed is the one
who trusts in the LORD,
who does not look to the proud,
to those who turn aside to false gods.
Many, LORD my God,
are the wonders you have done,
the things you planned for us.
None can compare with you;
were I to speak and tell of your deeds,
they would be too many to declare.

PSALM 40:1-5 NIV

*S*ometimes life feels like the "slimy pit" the psalmist describes. Do you feel like you're being held down by the "mud and mire" of life? Disappointments, frustrations, discouragement can swirl around us, weighing us down and stifling our joy. Those times can make it difficult to follow the command in 1 Thessalonians 5:18 to "give thanks in all circumstances" (NIV).

Several years ago, God used my child to drive home this point.

"Mom, did you thank God for your kidney infection?" There was my little eight-year-old daughter looking at me with those piercing blue eyes. Hmm. Had I thanked God for my kidney infection that was stabbing my side and sapping my energy? Uh, no! Then I remembered what I told my family the last time I had a kidney infection. As soon as I stopped being angry over the fact that I had yet another infection and asked God's help in obeying 1 Thessalonians 5:18 to "give thanks in all circumstances," I started feeling better. It's the Colossians 3:2 principle, "Set your minds on things above, not on earthly things" (NIV). When we cast our life in the big picture view that our heavenly Father sees, then our mood changes. Yes, there's still pain—but it feels more like pain with a purpose.

For several years during the time when my kids were young, those reoccurring painful, energy-zapping kidney infections were my slimy pit. But Psalm 40 would bring me hope. The Psalmist "waited patiently" and cried to God, and God heard him. I love the heartfelt transparency of this Psalm. He's thankful God has pulled him from the mud and given him a firm place to stand. He's thankful for the new song that God has put on his lips. He's thankful for the plans God has for him and that there are so many he can't even list them all.

I thought about this psalm as my family visited Rotterdam's city center in the Netherlands. My husband's extended family (who live in the Netherlands) explained that the heart of Rotterdam had been torn to shreds in World War 2. All that was left was the shell of a church. Yet, when we visited recently, rising from the "mud and mire" were new buildings. While the beautiful old buildings that dotted the landscape had been destroyed horrifically; today, in their place is a bastion of creativity. Whimsical, contemporary architecture dots the landscape, with colorful accents in yellow and burgundy brightening the sometimes gray skyline. One anything-but-ordinary apartment complex broke the mold by using visually compelling, yellow geometric shapes with corners that jut out. Another building was affectionately dubbed "the pencil" because of its pointy top, with curved windows and burgundy accents like pops of joy.

In what the psalmist might have called a "slimy pit" of "mud and mire," now stands a vibrant, unique community. As my family discussed how God can take what Satan means for evil and transform it for good (Genesis 50:20), my son shared about images popular on Pinterest that showcase the technique Kintsukuroi, also called Kintsugi. Instead of painstakingly gluing a broken pot back together so you can't see the damage, this Japanese tradition actually highlights the fractures by healing the break using very visible gold or silver lacquer. Instead of the damage diminishing its value, mending with Kintsugi actually increases the value and results in a product that is often more attractive than the original, unbroken piece.

What a beautiful picture of Romans 8:28, "And we know that in all things God works for the good of those who love him, who have been called according to his purpose" (NIV). How might God be healing your brokenness in ways that will be beneficial and compelling? How might God be pulling you or a loved one up and out of a painful time?

Psalm 40:2-3 NIV

He lifted me out of the slimy pit,
    out of the mud and mire;
    he set my feet on a rock
and gave me a firm place to stand.
He put a new song in my mouth,
    a hymn of praise to our God.
Many will see and fear the LORD
    and put their trust in him.

Do those words give you hope? When we aim to "give thanks in all circumstances" (1 Thessalonians 5:18 NIV), we can look at our difficulties and be thankful knowing that God can transform today's pain and heartache into something beautiful.

Are you struggling to be thankful in all circumstances? Are you having a hard time remembering that God is working out a good plan? Meditate on these verses from 2 Corinthians 4:7-9 and 16-18: "We have this treasure in jars of clay to show that this all-surpassing power is from God and not from us. We are hard pressed on every side, but not crushed; perplexed, but not in despair; persecuted, but not abandoned; struck down, but not destroyed...

Therefore we do not lose heart. Though outwardly we are wasting away, yet inwardly we are being renewed day by day. For our light and momentary troubles are achieving for us an eternal glory that far outweighs them all. So we fix our eyes not on what is seen, but on what is unseen, since what is seen is temporary, but what is unseen is eternal" (NIV).

Praise

Lord, I praise You from Psalm 40 that You love to lift us out of the slimy pit, out of the mud and mire, and give us a firm place to stand. Many, Lord my God, are the wonders You have done, the things You planned for us.

Confession

Lord, forgive me for the times I do not wait patiently, for the times I wallow in the "mud and mire" and focus on the "slimy pit" instead of the good things You will create from this difficulty.

Thanksgiving

Psalm 40:5 says, "Many, LORD my God, are the wonders you have done, the things you planned for us. None can compare with you;

were I to speak and tell of your deeds, they would be too many to declare" (Psalm 40:5 NIV). Lord, I specifically thank You for...

· · · · · · · · · · · · · · · · · · Intercession · · · · · · · · · · · · · · · · · ·

Lord, help _____ wait patiently for You to deliver him/her. Set his/her feet on a rock and give him/her a firm place to stand. Put a new song in _____'s mouth, a song of praise to You, God, so that many will see and fear the Lord and put their trust in You.

FROM PSALM 40:1-3

· · · · · · · · · · · · · · · · · · Petition · · · · · · · · · · · · · · · · · ·

Lord, help me wait patiently for You, Lord. Turn to me and hear my cry. Lift me out of the slimy pit, out of the mud and mire; and set my feet on a rock and give me a firm place to stand. Put a new song in my mouth, a hymn of praise to You, God, so that many will see and fear the Lord and put their trust in You.

FROM PSALM 40:1-3

Empowered Through Intercession

Prayer is the avenue God has chosen to unleash His power to do His will. The fourth step of prayer, called *intercession*, focuses on praying for others, standing in the gap for those who need our prayers. How do we know God's will? By praying the Scriptures. Thus, we also incorporate praying the Scriptures for others. And, when we are filled with the Holy Spirit, our prayers are empowered by the wisdom of the Lord to pray in ways that we might not have originally intended. But when we allow the Holy Spirit to direct our prayers, we can impact a life, a community, and even the world.

> *This is the confidence we have in approaching God: that if we ask anything according to his will, he hears us. And if we know that he hears us—whatever we ask—we know that we have what we asked of him.*
>
> 1 JOHN 5:14-15 NIV

31

Learning That God Is Not a Genie in a Bottle

· · · · · · · · · · · · · · · · · · · Cyndie · · · · · · · · · · · · · · · · · ·

*"Therefore I tell you, do not worry about your life, what
you will eat or drink; or about your body, what you will
wear. Is not life more than food, and the body more than
clothes? Look at the birds of the air; they do not sow or reap
or store away in barns, and yet your heavenly Father feeds
them. Are you not much more valuable than they? Can
any one of you by worrying add a single hour to your life?*

*"And why do you worry about clothes? See how the flowers
of the field grow. They do not labor or spin. Yet I tell you
that not even Solomon in all his splendor was dressed like
one of these. If that is how God clothes the grass of the field,
which is here today and tomorrow is thrown into the fire,
will he not much more clothe you—you of little faith?"*

MATTHEW 6:25-30 NIV

S tanding on the playground in fourth grade, I looked up at the
beautiful blue sky during recess, and I began to pray—for rain.
My Sunday school teacher had shared the story of Elijah praying for
rain, and I thought, well, why not give it a try. If God made it rain for
Elijah, why not for me?

I became a Christian when I was just four years old thanks to a local
church that had a bus ministry that picked up me and my sisters every
Sunday and drove us to church. In my little pre-school Sunday school
class, I first heard about my need for a Savior to get to heaven because

we could never be good enough on our own. I have a vivid memory of the teacher's diagram of how we try to do good works yet fail because we aren't perfect. But Jesus is perfect. All I had to do was ask Him into my heart. Seemed easy enough. I went home, waited for a rare moment when my family of eight was not around, closed the door to the room that I shared with a couple other siblings, and prayed my first prayer, asking Jesus into my heart.

The more I went to Sunday school, the more I learned about God and prayer. By first grade, I fully believed God would answer all my prayers. In fact, I prayed that God would help me guess the number of beans in a large jar at school so I could win a huge wooden Santa Claus. The contest was for the entire elementary school, and I won! My little first-grade friends helped me haul ginormous Santa to my house, a few blocks away. While I was delighted, I certainly was not surprised. I prayed, and God answered. Isn't that the way it always works?

Fast forward to fourth grade. I was placed in a class with fifth and sixth graders. Maybe that was a good idea academically, but socially that was a bad fit. I became self-conscious, especially of my clothes. After all, I was the fourth daughter in a family of six children. I didn't have new clothes. Yet, I was surrounded by fifth- and sixth-grade girls who had begun to care about their appearance. Mind you, I was in fourth grade, so a weekly bathing was still just fine by me. But I began to notice others' nice outfits. In Sunday school, the teacher talked about Matthew 6:28-30, the opening verse for today's devotion. So, as the fairly obedient and quiet child that I was, I prayed, asking God to supply my clothing needs. Do you know the verse Ephesians 3:20 (NIV) that says that God is "able to do immeasurably more than all we ask or imagine"? Well, that's what God did for me. My sister's best friend had just outgrown her clothes, and she gave them to me! I was overjoyed to have such beautiful new clothes. I went two entire weeks without having to repeat a piece of clothing. (Although, one day, as I sported the most comfortable shirt and elastic-waist pants, a fellow-student commented how much my new outfit looked like her pajamas!)

Did God answer prayer? I had absolutely no doubt in my mind. So imagine my surprise when a few weeks later, I prayed for rain and there *was no rain!* I was miffed, spiritually insulted, and determined to figure out this prayer thing. After a little elementary-school level soul searching, I realized God wasn't like the genies on TV, especially the ones on the *I Dream of Jeanie* reruns I liked to watch. Hmm, so why did God answer my other big prayer requests but didn't let it pour down rain on the playground? Why does God shower me with answered prayers that are "more than all I ask or imagine" sometimes, and other times not? It took me awhile to realize...it's not all about me. Shocking, I know.

Reading the Bible every day and talking with God had changed my relationship with my heavenly Father from just asking for requests like He was a genie in a bottle, to that of a real relationship. Ah, that was the key! Prayer is not about presenting a list of requests, it's about growing closer to God and allowing God to transform us to mirror Jesus Christ. The big answer of prayer that led to my friends and I carrying a wooden Santa home wasn't about the contest at all, it was about God answering the cry of a child's heart so she knew that the Creator of the universe loved her, personally. Why did He answer my prayer for clothes? Of course, God loves to give good gifts to His children, but I think it was also because I was praying scriptures and claiming God's promise in Matthew 6:28-30. And why didn't He let it pour rain on a beautiful Southern California day just because I had asked? That was purely an intellectual prayer request. It wasn't heartfelt. I wasn't praying according to God's will. It was a child asking for, in essence, a magic trick. As I steadily read the Bible, God gave me a deeper understanding of prayer with verses like 1 John 5:14-15, "This is the confidence we have in approaching God: that if we ask anything according to his will, he hears us. And if we know that he hears us—whatever we ask—we know that we have what we asked of him" (NIV).

••••••••••••••••••••••••••••••

Prayer is not about presenting a list of
requests, it's about growing closer to God.

••••••••••••••••••••••••••••••

Soon, I realized that the power in prayer isn't just for me: It can be a life-transforming gift I pour out on others, even without them knowing. I have witnessed God answer intercessory prayers for others over and over again and many times without the person even knowing I was praying. As we stand in the gap for others in prayer, God loves to answer in His perfect timing and according to His perfect will. Sometimes we get to witness God performing the miraculous transformation (like He did with my niece, as I share later in Chapter 33). Other times we might never know this side of heaven how a chorus of prayers buoyed someone who was down, prevented a tragedy, breathed peace into a chaotic situation, or brought someone to salvation in Christ.

Is a colleague having a bad day? Does the cashier seem gloomy? Is the school crossing guard frustrated? Pray for them. Remember, God can hear our prayers as we intercede for others.

Who do you know that needs your prayers? Who needs to have scriptural and Holy Spirit-directed prayers poured into their lives and into their circumstances? Throughout the day, remember to intercede for those around you, and watch with expectation how God will answer in His perfect timing, in His perfect way.

· · · · · · · · · · · · · · · · · · **Praise** · · · · · · · · · · · · · · · · · ·

*Lord, I praise You for caring about the details of
our lives, like our clothing, and for allowing us the
privilege to intercede in prayer for others.*

· · · · · · · · · · · · · · · · · **Confession** · · · · · · · · · · · · · · · · ·

*Forgive me for the times I worry and fret about
things like food and clothing, instead of trusting
that You will take care of my every need.*

· · · · · · · · · · · · · · · · **Thanksgiving** · · · · · · · · · · · · · · · ·

Thank You for always providing for my needs.
Specifically, Lord, thank You for...

· · · · · · · · · · · · · · · · **Intercession** · · · · · · · · · · · · · · · ·

Lord, I pray _____ will not worry about what he/
she will eat or drink; or about what he/she will wear.

FROM MATTHEW 6:25

· · · · · · · · · · · · · · · · **Petition** · · · · · · · · · · · · · · · ·

Oh Lord, help me not to worry about what I'll eat or
drink; or what I will wear in this situation...

FROM MATTHEW 6:25

32

Praying God's Will

*Pray, then, in this way: "Our Father who is in
heaven, Hallowed be Your name. Your kingdom
come. Your will be done, on earth as it is in heaven."*

MATTHEW 6:9-10

*P*rayer is the most powerful weapon or tool we have here on earth.
It can unleash God's power to do His perfect will as we pray. And
nothing is greater than His power. Remember He spoke this world into
being. Just by His word it was all accomplished. No power compares
to this. Revelation 4:11 says, "Worthy are You, our Lord and our God,
to receive glory and honor and power; for You created all things, and
because of Your will they existed, and were created."

And if we pray His word it does not come back void. It will accomplish God's will, for His word is His will.

Isaiah 55:8-11

"For My thoughts are not your thoughts, nor are your
ways My ways," declares the LORD.
"FOR *as* the heavens are higher than the earth,
So are My ways higher than your ways
And My thoughts than your thoughts.
For as the rain and the snow come down from heaven,
And do not return there without watering the earth

And making it bear and sprout,
And furnishing seed to the sower
and bread to the eater;
So will My word be which goes forth from My mouth;
It will not return to Me empty,
Without accomplishing what I desire."

The greatest prayer we can pray, whether for ourselves or when we intercede for others, is that God's will be done on earth as it is in heaven.

This prayer will unleash God's power to destroy and defeat all that stands against you. It will enable you to walk empowered by His Spirit and to accomplish more than you could ever ask or imagine. As we surrender our will to God's, we can walk empowered with peace, joy, confidence, and with all we need for life and godliness. Each step is set before us.

> "Not by might nor by power, but by My Spirit," says the LORD of hosts (Zechariah 4:6).

> For we are God's workmanship created in Christ Jesus to do good works which God prepared in advance for us to do (Ephesians 2:10 NKJV).

> Many, LORD my God, are the wonders you have done, the things you planned for us. None can compare with you; were I to speak and tell of your deeds, they would be too many to declare (Psalm 40:5 NIV).

> Just as it is written, "THINGS WHICH EYE HAS NOT SEEN AND EAR HAS NOT HEARD, AND *which* HAVE NOT ENTERED THE HEART OF MAN, ALL THAT GOD HAS PREPARED FOR THOSE WHO LOVE HIM" (1 Corinthians 2:9).

I know without a shadow of a doubt that God has a mighty plan for your life and for your loved ones. Our part is a surrendered heart to hear Him say, "This is the way; walk in it" (Isaiah 30:21).

Jesus is our living example of what it is to walk here on this earth with a powerful calling and a surrendered heart. There were times when Jesus needed to get His heart entwined with God's heart: He had to surrender His will to God's. He did this through prayer. If Jesus needed time to align His heart with God, so do we.

The disciples witnessed Jesus empowered by God to walk in peace, purpose, wisdom, and strength. No wonder they asked Him to teach them to pray.

If you want to walk empowered by the Holy Spirit to fulfill God's amazing calling on your life, you must get in such a place that you have no will of your own, but only the will of your Father.

Luke 22:39-43

> He came out and proceeded as was His custom to the Mount of Olives; and the disciples also followed Him. When He arrived at the place (Garden of Gethsemane), He said to them, "Pray that you may not enter into temptation." And He withdrew from them about a stone's throw, and He knelt down and began to pray, saying, "Father, if You are willing, remove this cup from Me; yet not My will, but Yours be done." Now an angel from heaven appeared to Him, strengthening Him.

You and I will never have to face what Jesus did. He was called to die for all mankind, to take the weight of all our sin upon Him. Yet we are called to bring glory to God, impacting our world for Christ. That is a great calling that only God can do through us.

· ·

It Jesus needed time to align His
heart with God, so do we.

· ·

The disciples would face tremendous trials and tribulations. Through it all they considered it pure joy, continually strengthening

and praying for others. Each disciple, except Judas, fulfilled God's calling on their lives, which brought God glory and impacted our world
for Christ. Their lives still touch ours today.

The secret to their empowered life is seen in the Lord's prayer: "Your
kingdom come. Your will be done, on earth as it is in heaven." It is not
something to just repeat over and over again. It is not something to
wish for the future, it is to be lived out today in your life.

In Luke 17, as the people of God were asking Jesus when the kingdom of God would come, He answered, "Now having been questioned
by the Pharisees as to when the kingdom of God was coming, He
answered them and said, 'The kingdom of God is not coming with
signs to be observed; nor will they say, "Look, here it is!" or, "There it
is!" For behold, the kingdom of God is in your midst'" (Luke 17:20-
21). In the footnotes of my Bible it offers this translation alternative to
"in your midst": "is within you."

They were looking for an earthly kingdom that had the power to set
them free from their enemies. And Jesus was sharing with them something greater: a kingdom of God that would defeat all our enemies, and
its power was standing right there in their midst. They were looking for
an earthly kingdom. Yet God wanted to give them a heavenly kingdom.

"Blessed are the poor in spirit, for theirs is the kingdom of heaven"
(Matthew 5:3). It is the humble of heart, the one who is dependent on
God, who will be empowered by heaven. The Pharisees were the oppo-
site, and their prayers had no power.

For Christians, Jesus lives within us. "In Him all the fullness of
Deity dwells in bodily form, and in Him you have been made complete,
and He is the head over all rule and authority" (Colossians 2:9-10).

And only Christ in us can accomplish His mighty will.

> It is God who is at work in you, both to will and to work
> for His good pleasure (Philippians 2:13).

> To Him who is able to do far more abundantly beyond
> all that we ask or think, according to the power that
> works within us (Ephesians 3:20).

So my prayer for myself and for you is that day by day, moment by moment, you will surrender your will to live out His!

· · · · · · · · · · · · · · · · · **Praise** · · · · · · · · · · · · · · · · ·

I ascribe to You LORD the glory due Your name;
I worship You LORD in the splendor of Your holiness.

FROM PSALM 29:2

· · · · · · · · · · · · · · · · **Confession** · · · · · · · · · · · · · · · ·

Forgive me for being stubborn and not surrendering my
will to You. Forgive me when I take for granted my daily
bread, not only food for my body, but the food for my soul!

· · · · · · · · · · · · · · · **Thanksgiving** · · · · · · · · · · · · · · ·

Thank You that through Your Word I can know Your will.

· · · · · · · · · · · · · · · · **Intercession** · · · · · · · · · · · · · · · ·

Fill _____ with the knowledge of Your will through
all the wisdom and understanding that the Spirit gives,
so that _____ will live a life worthy of You. May
_____ please You in every way: bearing fruit in
every good work, growing in the knowledge of God.

FROM COLOSSIANS 1:9-10

•••••••••••••••••• **Petition** ••••••••••••••••••

Lord, fill me with the knowledge of Your will through all the wisdom and understanding that the Spirit gives, so that I will live a life worthy of You. May I please You in every way: bearing fruit in every good work, growing in the knowledge of God.

FROM COLOSSIAN 1:9-10

33

More Than All We Ask or Imagine

········· Cyndie ·········

*Now to him who is able to do immeasurably more than all
we ask or imagine, according to his power that is at work
within us, to him be glory in the church and in Christ
Jesus throughout all generations, for ever and ever! Amen.*

EPHESIANS 3:20-21 NIV

Do you have my daddy?" my sweet little niece looked at me with
her big brown eyes. How do you tell a toddler that her daddy,
my brother, was in prison, holed up in "segregation" for starting a
fight among inmate gang members, and he wasn't allowed visitors? Her
words rang in my ears over and over. "Do you have my daddy?" Oh,
how I wished I did. Her little sister barely even knew her dad, who was
first incarcerated when she was just a few months old. Sadly, most of
her daddy time was spent in a secure visitation room.

I adored my two little nieces, treasuring every weekend and evening
I could spend with them. So when my brother's messy divorce meant
my time with the girls was limited, my heart ached to see them again.

Sometimes in the darkness, the only ray of light comes from prayer.
I held onto the promises of the Lord. Praying the Scriptures meant I
was praying God's words back to Him. And boy did I pray! I clung to
Ephesians 3:20 that God is able to do immeasurably more than all I
asked or imagined. And as I prayed for the Holy Spirit to grab hold of
my brother's heart and transform his life, I also prayed for my nieces.
I prayed they would be able to step outside their family lineage and

graduate from high school. I prayed they would come to love God and follow Him.

One day, as I accepted a collect call from my brother from prison, I was prepared to encourage my brother, who had been quite sad since his divorce. But instead, he encouraged me! He was excitedly sharing that He had come to Christ and experienced a miracle. A severe learning disability had made it hard for him to read. Even as he studied to try to pass his high school equivalency exam, he continued to bomb the reading comprehension portion. But as he prayed to God, he asked Him to lift the veil from his eyes and allow him to read the Holy Scriptures.

....

Sometimes in the darkness, the only
ray of light comes from prayer.

....

What followed was nothing short of a miracle! He said it was like scales falling off his eyes, and suddenly the words of the Bible began to come to life. What once was agonizingly painful, had become a joy. And the next time he took the high school equivalency exam, he passed with flying colors, receiving 99 percent in his reading comprehension!

Fast forward almost 20 years, and my brother—who had struggled to read throughout his childhood—sailed through college and seminary (yes, seminary!) and became the pastor of a church in the very same neighborhood that he once terrorized as a gang member. His powerful testimony and life illustrations were never lost on his congregation.

God answered our prayers for my brother in surprising ways that were truly more than all we asked or imagined. For my nieces, though, I soon found out I hadn't "imagined" big enough prayer requests.

Both nieces grew into lovely young, responsible women who graduated from high school. The youngest one used to enjoy partying before becoming a busy single mom, working full-time and caring for her adorable curly-haired son. Reading the Bible or going to church was not on her radar until a restaurant owner displayed little invites to his church. But though she had noticed the invites, she never even thought to pick one up until her friend came into town and, on a whim, suggested they attend church. After stopping by the restaurant to grab the little invite card, she and her friend unknowingly followed God's path straight into His loving hands.

Even on the first visit, she realized the church had something she was missing. Soon she was attending Sundays, Wednesdays, and helping in the nursery. The difference in her clothing choices, social media posts, and, well, let's say "colorful language" was striking. When she had a conflict at work, she thought, "How would God feel about how I'm acting?" That was convicting to her and she began to reach out to her colleagues in love. When she started acting nice to them, they, in turn, softened to her.

Then her church started taking signups for a summer mission trip. As a mom of a toddler, she thought there was no way she could go to Guatemala to build homes and encourage other single moms. But God started tugging at her heart, and He worked out all the details for her son to enjoy cousin time while she was serving for the week.

Then, she took the plunge and was baptized! Tears streamed down my face as her pastor said, "Two important questions: I know the answers already. Do you love Jesus Christ with all your heart? Do you promise to serve Him all the days of your life?" I was filled with joy knowing that the pastor of this large church already knew my niece's heart after she had been following Christ for only 10 months. My gratitude overflowed considering what God had done to transform her heart and empower her to do His will.

A couple decades ago, I would have never, ever guessed my brother would be a pastor or my niece would be such a Jesus follower that she would go on a short-term mission trip. But God is truly able to do "more than all we ask or imagine," as Ephesians 3:20 says.

What prayer request tugs at your heart as being impossible? Have you given up praying? Ecclesiastes 3:11 says, "He has made everything beautiful in its time." Keep persevering in prayer and see how God will answer in ways that are more than all you ask or imagine.

Praise

*Lord, we praise You that You are the God of miracles,
that You delight in answering our prayers in ways that
are much more than we ask or even imagine.*

Confession

*Lord, forgive my unbelieving heart. Help me to
persevere in prayer even when hope seems invisible.*

Thanksgiving

*Oh, how I thank You for the amazing ways You answer
prayer in Your perfect timing. Thank You for transforming
lives, and for what You are doing in _____'s life.*

Intercession

*I pray You will do "immeasurably more than all we ask
or imagine" in the life of _____. Lord, please
show up in a miraculous way, and help me to be
persistent and bold in my prayers for him/her.*

FROM EPHESIANS 3:20

Petition

*Now to You who are able to do immeasurably more than all
we ask or imagine, according to Your power that is at work
within us, to You be glory in the church and in Christ Jesus
throughout all generations, for ever and ever! Amen.*

FROM EPHESIANS 3:20-21

34

Just Keep Praying

*Then, teaching them more about prayer, he [Jesus] used this
story: "Suppose you went to a friend's house at midnight,
wanting to borrow three loaves of bread. You say to him,
'A friend of mine has just arrived for a visit, and I have
nothing for him to eat.' And suppose he calls out from his
bedroom, 'Don't bother me. The door is locked for the night,
and my family and I are all in bed. I can't help you.' But I
tell you this—though he won't do it for friendship's sake, if
you keep knocking long enough, he will get up and give you
whatever you need because of your shameless persistence.*

*"And so I tell you, keep on asking, and you will receive
what you ask for. Keep on seeking, and you will find. Keep
on knocking, and the door will be opened to you. For
everyone who asks, receives. Everyone who seeks, finds.
And to everyone who knocks, the door will be opened."*

LUKE 11:5-10 NLT

A dear person asked me recently if I was going to put him in my
next book. He is in his fifties, addicted to alcohol and drugs, and
has been in and out of rehabs. The list of his troubles goes on: He's in
a heap of trouble with the law, finances, and his second failed marriage. The troubles he has brought on himself have also hurt the people
around him, including his precious children. My first reaction to his

question was that I would gladly tell his story once he was redeemed! And yet his story must be told.

Are you ready to give up on a friend or a loved one in the same situation? You think God is never going to bring that person to Jesus. And yet we read the scripture above and realize God does not want us to give up. He wants us to keep praying.

God has strategically placed this person in your life so you will pray, and so you, too, will be transformed. With every prayer you pray, God is moving in you, transforming you, and giving you hope you didn't know you had. He is moving in the situation that seems impossible, bringing His redeeming power. "For nothing will be impossible with God" (Luke 1:37).

Luke 18:25-27

> "Indeed, it is easier for a camel to go through the eye of a needle than for someone who is rich to enter the kingdom of God." Those who heard this asked, "Who then can be saved?" Jesus replied, "What is impossible with man is possible with God" (NIV).

These past few years we have seen the impossible done with many of our loved ones. Because of addiction, a precious loved one lost the custody of her young children. I remember praying for her for years and years. All I had was a mustard seed of faith.

Matthew 17:20

> He said to them, "Because of the littleness of your faith; for truly I say to you, if you have faith the size of a mustard seed, you will say to this mountain, 'Move from here to there,' and it will move; and nothing will be impossible to you."

God, who kept me praying for her for years, answered those prayers with her receiving Jesus as her Lord and Savior. Her children, years later, are now back with her. God reconciled them and they go to church together. She told me, "Thank you for continuing to pray for me and not giving up." I almost did several times, yet God stirred me to continue. Even with a mustard seed of faith, I prayed.

The following year, we witnessed another loved one come to know the Lord. And this year yet another. All three of these friends seemed unlikely candidates to be the first in their families to surrender to Jesus. Each could be the perfect picture of the woman at the well in John 4. God reached out to each one of them and they took a drink of His living water! "Whoever drinks of the water that I will give him shall never thirst; but the water that I will give him will become in him a well of water springing up to eternal life" (John 4:14).

And when I become discouraged or weary of praying for someone, I remember this truth about our God: "The Lord is not slow about His promise, as some count slowness, but is patient toward you, not wishing for any to perish but for all to come to repentance" (2 Peter 3:9).

It is God who draws man to Himself. When we pray and share God's Word, He uses us as His vessels...we get to be part of the impossible.

I remember standing in a low-security prison, getting ready to share the gospel with about 75 prisoners. The prisoners were large, strong women, dressed in orange. They were hardened by sorrows and darkness: some they caused and some were done to them. I shared the gospel loud and clear. I once was in darkness and knew they needed the light of the gospel. And as I closed my eyes and invited them to pray with me, voices rang out, tears streamed down their faces. Those of us who were a part of the ministry team stood amazed at what God did that night. As we left and drove back down the hill, we were silent in our thoughts of the miracle God brought to these women. I thanked the Lord for the hope of Romans 1:16, "I am not ashamed of the gospel, for it is the power of God for salvation to everyone who believes, to the Jew first and also to the Greek."

• •

When we pray and share God's Word, He uses us
as His vessels...we get to be part of the impossible.

• •

For more than 30 years I have witnessed God do the impossible as we pray. I have seen Him move in marriages, jobs, health and many other things. You may be struggling or maybe your family is in the midst of an impossible trial. I ask you to keep on praying and never give up. Remember Philippians 1:6, "I am confident of this very thing, that He who began a good work in you will perfect it until the day of Christ Jesus."

················· Praise ·················

Lord, I praise You. Nothing is impossible with You and what is impossible with man is possible with You, God. And Your power is unleashed every time I pray. You desire that none should perish!

FROM LUKE 1:37 AND LUKE 18:1

················· Confession ·················

Lord, forgive me as I am of little faith and want to give up. My weariness and frustration with the world is causing me to question Your strength, resilience, and power. Give me faith in Your redeeming power.

················· Thanksgiving ·················

Lord, I thank You for Your promise in Hebrews 4:16, "Let us draw near with confidence to the throne of grace, so that we may receive mercy and find grace to help in time of need."

················· Intercession ·················

Lord, help _____'s unbelief! Help him/her to keep praying, never giving up! You love _____'s loved one more than any person could, and You wish no one should perish.

· · · · · · · · · · · · · · · · · · **Petition** · · · · · · · · · · · · · · · · · ·

Lord I believe. Help my unbelief! Help me to keep praying, never giving up! You love my loved one more than I do and You wish no one should perish. So, Lord, hear my prayer for _____. Bring him/her to the saving knowledge of Your mercy and grace.

35

The Ache Is in the Waiting

.... Cyndie ....

Wait for the LORD;
Be strong and let your heart take courage;
Yes, wait for the LORD.

PSALM 27:14

The ache lives at the end of each breath. Sure, you still smile and even laugh. But on each exhale, where the heart meets the stomach, meets the lungs, a stab of pain resides. Waiting—with all the questions, unknowns and what-ifs—can be uncomfortably bloated with stagnant, agonizing pain. It tests our stamina, courage, and perseverance. But whether we await a diagnosis, a resolution, a new job, or the answer to a long-standing prayer request, our hope in the Lord is the hand that pulls us forward. That hope keeps us on our knees and our eyes on the Lord. Hope reminds us there's a bigger picture. Hope motivates us to keep going when all we want to do is sit and think and cry.

As I write this, my heart aches for my niece who lies on a hospital bed, having finished a blood transfusion after her appendix didn't just burst but disintegrated. During the exploratory surgery, they found pieces of her appendix attached to parts of her intestines where they had no business being. She could have died. Is she out of the woods, yet? Has the infection calmed down? The ache is in the waiting.

At the same time, my mom is on the verge of a battery of cardiac tests. Is it congestive heart failure? Is it a faulty heart valve? Would she outlive all her siblings, or would this be her last year before being reunited in heaven with her husband of 35 years?

And we wait.

The very same week, my brother went to the ER for a possible heart attack. Tests are inconclusive. So, again, we wait.

••••••••••••••••••••••••••••••

Hope reminds us there's a bigger picture.

••••••••••••••••••••••••••••••

"Wait for the Lord; be strong and take heart and wait for the Lord" (Psalm 27:14).

The feeling of concern and wanting to do something where there's nothing to be done drew me to my quiet time. I yearned to bring every care and concern to the Lord, to pour out my heart before the God who hears and cares.

In the early morning, before the household stirred, I tiptoed down to my special quiet time chair ready to pour out my heart to God. As I opened my Bible, I read "offering of thanks…" Ah, yes, I needed to start with not only thanksgiving, but also praise and confession. And so I began.

> Lord, I praise You for being loving and trustworthy. Because I know You love not only me but each of my family members, I can trust You. I know that You are working out a bigger plan that I can't see right now. Lord, forgive me for my worry and anxiety. I give those to You so that You can fill me with Your inexplicable peace. And oh how thankful I am that my niece's life was saved and that You know exactly what is happening with my mom and brother's health—even if tests are inconclusive for both right now. Lord, help each one in my family as we wait for You. Help us to be strong and take heart and wait. May we not go out ahead of Your will, but may it all be in Your perfect timing. Give wisdom to the

doctors for my niece, my brother and my mom. Bring healing to them so they can live out Your good purpose in their lives. Provide for the financial assistance in covering for my niece's hospital stay and all the testing (which God did miraculously!). We trust in Your good purpose and power.

Suddenly, I could feel the peace of God buoy me. But when the bits of worry come back, I go through the four steps again. And when each text message brings more updates, I again bring each concern to the Lord.

My social media account reminds me that it was about a year ago when I wrestled with waiting for results from my daughter's MRI. She had hurt her back working on some aggressive choreography for a dance duet for her and her friend. Unfortunately, it was right at the beginning of the high school's competitive dance season. She wouldn't miss a competition, but instead powered through the pain. After the season, one doctor appointment led to an X-ray, which led to another doctor appointment, which led to an MRI. With all that waiting, she had decided she was fine. Too bad the doctor didn't agree!

Before we finally had the appointment with the orthopedic specialist, my daughter had assured me she was okay. So, we made arrangements with friends to take summer dance intensives. She explored colleges with dance teams and began to consider a degree in dance education.

However, after the doctor examined her, he put her on a no-dancing restriction and diagnosed her with a "stress fracture" in a spot along her spinal column. *A stress fracture? You mean a broken back? Wait. That sounds so serious!* I wrote this the next day:

> As I sit here the morning after, the wave of disappointment for my daughter washes over me. She LOVES to perform. She LIVES to move. And she's been dancing and kicking from the time she was in utero. Her latest goal was to find a competitive dance team in college, and

she was ready to spend the summer in intensive classes
to get her skills ready for the auditions that would come
in two years. But then… rest. And will there be more?
Will she need a brace? Or surgery? Will she dance again?

We had a choice: to stress and worry, or to follow Psalm 27:14, "Wait
for the LORD; be strong and take heart and wait for the LORD" (NIV).

So, again, we aimed to follow the command in 1 Peter 5:7 to cast all
our anxiety on the Lord, because he cares for us. And, again, as always,
God made Himself known. After about two months of no dancing,
my daughter was able to slowly start dancing again, and—as only God
can do —she didn't miss a single performance her junior year due to
injury. But was that the end of her injuries? No, God continues to give
her opportunities to "be strong and take heart and wait for the LORD."

As Ecclesiastes 3:11 says, "He has made everything beautiful in
its time" (NIV). Our Lord understands the ache of waiting and will
empower us to persevere through it if we just wait for Him. Will God's
plan always bring us exactly what we want? No. But we can trust that
He has a good and loving purpose for us, and He will reveal it in His
perfect timing.

· · · · · · · · · · · · · · · · · · · **Praise** · · · · · · · · · · · · · · · · · ·

*Lord, I praise You that Your timing is always perfect, and
that You do make everything beautiful in its own time.*

· · · · · · · · · · · · · · · · **Confession** · · · · · · · · · · · · · · · ·

*Lord, forgive me for the times I stress out and forget
to trust You while I'm in the place of waiting.*

Thanksgiving

I thank You, Lord, that You provide sweetness on the other side of the sour waiting period. Lord, thank You that we can carry each burden to You and intercede on behalf of others. Thank You that Your timing is always perfect.

Intercession

Lord, help _____ wait for You. Help him/her be strong and take heart and wait for You.

FROM PSALM 27:14

Petition

Lord, I find it hardest to wait in the area of _____. But Lord, I know You can help me as I wait. Lord, help me be strong and take heart and wait for You.

FROM PSALM 27:14

36

Praying for Our Enemies

· · · · · · · · · · · · · · · · · · · Sally · · · · · · · · · · · · · · · · · · ·

"You have heard that it was said, 'YOU SHALL LOVE YOUR NEIGHBOR and hate your enemy.' But I say to you, love your enemies and pray for those who persecute you, so that you may be sons of your Father who is in heaven."

MATTHEW 5:43-45

I have seen a weaker believer or unbeliever cause a strong believer to stumble through a war of words or actions. As believers, we must realize that the battle is not against flesh and blood. Ephesians 6:12 says, "Our struggle is not against flesh and blood, but against the rulers, against the powers, against the world forces of this darkness, against the spiritual forces of wickedness in the heavenly places."

We will not win by using weapons that attack the flesh. One can try to prove their accuser wrong and use all the power of man, but God has something so powerful it will bring down every stronghold and every weapon formed against you. "Though we walk in the flesh, we do not war according to the flesh, for the weapons of our warfare are not of the flesh, but divinely powerful for the destruction of fortresses. We are destroying speculations and every lofty thing raised up against the knowledge of God, and we are taking every thought captive to the obedience of Christ" (2 Corinthians 10:3-5).

It is through prayer the battle is won. It is through prayer we can stand firm in the will of God. It is in dying to self and praying for even your enemy that God will bring victory.

As a grandmother was praying for her grandson who had autism, he would call her with updates and prayer requests. He was doing well in high school, but one day he shared with his grandmother how a boy was bullying him. So this wise grandmother shared with her grandson that he should pray for this bully. He was not to say anything mean back or do anything in retaliation. When the grandson went to college, his bully was there too. Instead of bullying him, he asked the grandson for forgiveness and if he could go to Bible study with him. Prayer is more powerful than any enemy.

....

It is through prayer that the battle is won.

....

At one time you and I were God's enemy and yet He rescued us and made us His co-laborer in His kingdom! Should we not want the same for our enemies?

Romans 5:9-11

Much more then, having now been justified by His blood, we shall be saved from the wrath of God through Him. For if while we were enemies we were reconciled to God through the death of His Son, much more, having been reconciled, we shall be saved by His life. And not only this, but we also exult in God through our Lord Jesus Christ, through whom we have now received the reconciliation.

Through Moms in Prayer, I have witnessed how prayer is greater than our words or actions. We don't gossip about a teacher, student, or administrator: instead, we pray. We only have one hour to pray for our children and schools. So that does not leave time for talking about our worries or fears or dislikes on the school campus. Instead, we pray scriptures and a blessing upon each one at our school campuses throughout the year.

Just the other day I heard of another teacher we prayed for who had surrendered her life to God. She is the thirteenth teacher at that school! She retired several years ago, but our prayers never end until God answers them according to His will and purposes.

Many years earlier, a mom thanked God that her son made it home safely after running away from his classroom in fear of this teacher. He was not the first elementary student to run in fear of her. Now nothing negative was said about her, but we did pray for her salvation throughout the years, and, of course, that she would have a gentle heart toward the children. What a great privilege it is to intercede for every teacher. And we should. Teachers will influence the students of the campus. In fact, teachers will influence a generation.

Our flesh may want to pray the worst on others, but God has a greater plan. What if they became your brother or sister and prayed with you? Just recently, years after my children had left this school, I was invited to pray with a group of the teachers I witnessed "turn from darkness to light." They invited me one Saturday to a home of another teacher. They were battling in prayer for the life of a fellow teacher who had cancer. I would much rather battle with them than against them.

This elementary teacher who had put fear in her students recently came to know Jesus. After a heart attack, she went to her neighbor's house and said, "I need to get right with God. Can I come to your Bible study?" It was there she came to know Jesus. This woman, who once instilled fear upon children, had the fear of God put upon her. She passed away recently and now is with Jesus. And I am filled with joy that she became right with God before her passing.

A few decades ago, a mom showed me a picture of her wayward son. He had piercings and tattoos all over him. She said she was in a group of moms that prayed for the prodigal children who had turned away from God. Several of them had prayed that their children would be caught by the police so they would not be killed by drug dealers. This mom confidently prayed that when her son came back to the Lord he would be on fire. I agreed with the prayer because I knew God could do the impossible. And God answered her prayers. After her son returned to the Lord, he went to the mission fields of India and married a pastor's daughter. His whole family served faithfully in India before coming back to the USA where he is a full-time pastor at a large church.

She was sharing with me how surprised she was that the enemy was using people of the church to whisper falsehoods about him. The very people he was serving were hurling insults. Her greatest weapon to protect her son had not changed: She prayed!

Ephesians 6:10-11,18

> Finally, be strong in the Lord and in the strength of His might. Put on the full armor of God, so that you will be able to stand firm against the schemes of the devil... With all prayer and petition pray at all times in the Spirit, and with this in view, be on the alert with all perseverance and petition for all the saints.

Those who come against us—and many will—must use the mighty weapon of prayer: praying God's Word. Instead of speaking out against your enemies, begin to pray for them and let God move in their lives. You will use different scriptures for different people. For example, you might pray for an unbeliever Acts 26:18, that God will "open their eyes so that they may turn from darkness to light and from the dominion of Satan to God, that they may receive forgiveness of sins and an inheritance among those who have been sanctified by faith."

When praying for a believer, you might use Philippians 1:9-11: "This I pray, that your love may abound still more and more in real knowledge and all discernment, so that you may approve the things that are excellent, in order to be sincere and blameless until the day of Christ; having been filled with the fruit of righteousness which comes through Jesus Christ, to the glory and praise of God."

There may be times when you encounter a believer who has unwittingly come against you. You should talk to them face to face. You will want to speak the truth in love. "Yet do not regard him as an enemy, but admonish him as a brother" (2 Thessalonians 3:15).

No matter who comes against you, understand the battle is not yours but the Lord's. Our weapon for victory will only be found when we are on our knees.

Praise

I praise You that You loved the whole world and sent Your one and only Son to die for us all. You desire that none should perish but all come to repentance. And You are a God who is longsuffering. I praise You, Lord, for Your infinite love and patience for the people here on earth.

FROM JOHN 3:16

Confession

Oh Lord, I ask for forgiveness when I do not live a life worthy of the calling I have received. And forgive me when I am not completely humble and gentle; when I'm not being patient, or bearing with one another in love.

Thanksgiving

Thank You, Lord, for bringing into my life this challenging person, _____. I know You are teaching me how to love them like You do. And I thank You for the gift and the power of praying for them.

· · · · · · · · · · · **Intercession for a Believer** · · · · · · · · · · ·

*And this I pray, that _____'s love may abound still
more and more in real knowledge and all discernment, so
that _____ may approve the things that are excellent, in
order to be sincere and blameless until the day of Christ;
having been filled with the fruit of righteousness which
comes through Jesus Christ, to the glory and praise of God.*

FROM PHILIPPIANS 1:9-11

· · · · **Intercession for Those Who Don't Yet Believe** · · · ·

*May You, Lord, open _____'s eyes so that they may turn
from darkness to light and from the dominion of Satan to God,
that they may receive forgiveness of sins and an inheritance
among those who have been sanctified by faith in Jesus.*

FROM ACTS 26:18

· · · · · · · · · · · · · · · · · · **Petition** · · · · · · · · · · · · · · · · · ·

*Lord, help my love to abound still more and more in real
knowledge and all discernment, so that I may approve the things
that are excellent, in order to be sincere and blameless until the
day of Christ; having been filled with the fruit of righteousness
which comes through Jesus Christ, to Your glory and praise.*

FROM PHILIPPIANS 1:9-11

37

Praying for More Than Wealth and Success

· · · · · · · · · · · · · · · · · · ·▸ Cyndie ◂· · · · · · · · · · · · · · · · · · ·

*That night God appeared to Solomon and said, "What
do you want? Ask, and I will give it to you!"*

*Solomon replied to God, "You showed great and faithful
love to David, my father, and now you have made me king
in his place. O LORD God, please continue to keep your
promise to David my father, for you have made me king
over a people as numerous as the dust of the earth! Give
me the wisdom and knowledge to lead them properly, for
who could possibly govern this great people of yours?"*

*God said to Solomon, "Because your greatest desire
is to help your people, and you did not ask for wealth,
riches, fame, or even the death of your enemies or a long
life, but rather you asked for wisdom and knowledge to
properly govern my people—I will certainly give you the
wisdom and knowledge you requested. But I will also
give you wealth, riches, and fame such as no other king
has had before you or will ever have in the future!"*

2 CHRONICLES 1:7-12 NLT

*I*magine if the Creator of the heavens and earth said to you, "What
do you want? Ask, and I will give it to you." After you regained
composure from the shock of that question, what would you ask
for? Would it be something for yourself? Your children? Your spouse?

Someone else? Would you pray for wealth? Or health? Or success? Or popularity? Or would you choose character, instead?

Would you ask for wisdom over wealth? Knowledge over being noticed? Harmony over health?

If you're a parent, don't you love to give gifts to your children and watch their eyes light up with delight? But if your children want a gift that will do them harm, do you still give it to them? No. And when they pout and cry or yell in response to the "no," what helps us hold our ground? The truth that we are doing all that we can to keep our children safe and grow their character.

Our heavenly Father isn't limited by lack of time or money. He could overindulge our requests every single time. But He doesn't. Why? Romans 5:3-5 says, "We can rejoice, too, when we run into problems and trials, for we know that they help us develop endurance. And endurance develops strength of character, and character strengthens our confident hope of salvation. And this hope will not lead to disappointment. For we know how dearly God loves us, because he has given us the Holy Spirit to fill our hearts with his love" (NLT).

Our heavenly Father wants to grow us and shape us to have the heart of Christ, so we can share His love with the world. He wants the same for our children. So, while you might be praying that your daughter gets on the sports team she wants or that your son can ask a girl to prom without his heart being broken, God is looking at a bigger picture. He is looking at your child's character. Those difficulties we try to protect them from could be the very lessons they need for a future struggle with greater consequences.

When we pray that our children will become more Christ-like, we are praying the heart of God. Look how God answered Solomon's request for wisdom and knowledge to lead the Israelites. First Kings 4:29 says, "God gave Solomon wisdom and very great insight, and a breadth of understanding as measureless as the sand on the seashore" (NIV).

••••••••••••••••••••••••••••••••

When we pray that our children will become more
Christlike, we are praying the heart of God.

••••••••••••••••••••••••••••••••

Imagine if we looked past our children's grades or success or circle of friends and began to pray earnestly for them to have God's wisdom, knowledge, and understanding. Imagine if we prayed for our loved ones to have godly character, that they would love God with all their heart, with all their soul, and with all their mind, as Jesus said in Matthew 22:37. Are those not requests that our Creator would love to answer in His perfect timing?

· · · · · · · · · · · · · · · · · · **Praise** · · · · · · · · · · · · · · · · · ·

Lord, we praise You that You love to grant us answers to our prayer requests. And we praise You that, in Your infinite wisdom, You do not always grant our prayer requests that our loved ones will avoid difficulties, because sometimes it is through those very difficulties that You help them grow in their character and Christ-likeness.

· · · · · · · · · · · · · · · · **Confession** · · · · · · · · · · · · · · · ·

Lord, forgive me for the times that I doubt You because of struggles You allow into our lives. Help me remember that You have a bigger view and You know what trials and difficulties are necessary now, because it will help prepare us in the future.

· · · · · · · · · · · · · · · **Thanksgiving** · · · · · · · · · · · · · · ·

Lord, thank You that You love my family and friends even more than I do, and that Romans 8:28 says that You can transform everything to work together for the good of those who love You and are called according to Your purpose. That is such a great comfort to me. Thank You!

· · · · · · · · · · · · · · · · · · **Intercession** · · · · · · · · · · · · · · · · ·

*Lord, I continually ask You to fill _____ with the knowledge
of Your will through all the wisdom and understanding that
the Spirit gives. May he/she live a life worthy of the Lord and
please You in every way: bearing fruit in every good work,
growing in the knowledge of God, being strengthened with
all power according to Your glorious might. May _____
have great endurance and patience and give joyful thanks
to You, our Father, who has rescued us from darkness and
brought us into Your kingdom, through the redemption and
forgiveness of sins available to us through Jesus Christ.*

FROM COLOSSIANS 1:9-14

· · · · · · · · · · · · · · · · · · **Petition** · · · · · · · · · · · · · · · · · ·

*I pray that You help me rejoice when I run into problems
and trials, knowing that they help us develop endurance.
And endurance develops my strength of character, and
character strengthens my confident hope of salvation. And
this hope will not lead to disappointment. For I know
how dearly You love me, because You have given me
the Holy Spirit to fill my heart with Your love.*

FROM ROMANS 5:3-5

38

Love Others as You Love Yourself

· · · · · · · · · · · · · · · · · Sally · · · · · · · · · · · · · · · · ·

You will receive power when the Holy Spirit has
come upon you; and you shall be My witnesses
both in Jerusalem, and in all Judea and Samaria,
and even to the remotest part of the earth.

ACTS 1:8

You may say you're powerless to do anything as you hear what governments are doing and the corruption that abounds. You may feel powerless as you see what is happening in your neighborhoods, cities, and states. You may also feel helpless with what is happening in your homes and churches.

You are not powerless.

Your voice will be heard as you cry out to God. Your voice has great power to impact a family, a village, a city, a state, a nation, and our world for Christ. Prayer is the avenue God has chosen to unleash His power to do His will.

I was recently in a room full of pastors. Several shared that they had lost hope for revival in our state and even in our country. Yet as they began to gather together and pray for government officials and to witness God's answers, hope of revival and spiritual awakening began to arise. Then they went and visited the state capital and the White House. As they prayed, God restored their hope. They found a remnant in the midst of the corruption, men and women like Daniel, Esther, Nehemiah, and others.

Remember when Abraham interceded on behalf of Sodom and Gomorrah?

> Abraham came near and said, "Will You indeed sweep away the righteous with the wicked? Suppose there are fifty righteous within the city; will You indeed sweep it away and not spare the place for the sake of the fifty righteous who are in it? Far be it from You to do such a thing, to slay the righteous with the wicked, so that the righteous and the wicked are treated alike. Far be it from You! Shall not the Judge of all the earth deal justly?" So the LORD said, "If I find in Sodom fifty righteous within the city, then I will spare the whole place on their account." And Abraham replied, "Now behold, I have ventured to speak to the Lord, although I am but dust and ashes. Suppose the fifty righteous are lacking five, will You destroy the whole city because of five?" And He said, "I will not destroy it if I find forty-five there."...Then he said, "Oh may the Lord not be angry, and I shall speak only this once; suppose ten are found there?" And He said, "I will not destroy it on account of the ten." As soon as He had finished speaking to Abraham the Lord departed, and Abraham returned to his place (Genesis 18:23-28,32-33).

Because of Abraham's intercession, the Lord continued to reduce the number of righteous needed to thwart the destruction, down from 50 to only 10 righteous! We are never righteous on our own, only through Jesus! "Even the righteousness of God through faith in Jesus Christ for all those who believe; for there is no distinction; for all have sinned and fall short of the glory of God" (Romans 3:22-23).

That group of pastors I was with has found many who are righteous in places of government and are praying for revival and spiritual awakening to occur. It is amazing to see their transformation from being hopeless to having a great and active hope. Why did this change happen? Because they turned to God and prayed.

No wonder God tells us, "First of all, then, I urge that entreaties and prayers, petitions and thanksgivings, be made on behalf of all men, for kings and all who are in authority, so that we may lead a tranquil and quiet life in all godliness and dignity. This is good and acceptable in the sight of God our Savior" (1Timothy 2:1-3).

You and I can go from powerlessness—from fear and worry of things like governments that are out of our control—to being empowered with peace and prayer.

Any revival that has ever happened in any land has come through prayer. Second Chronicles 7:14 says, "My people who are called by My name humble themselves and pray and seek My face and turn from their wicked ways, then I will hear from heaven, will forgive their sin and will heal their land."

....

Your voice has great power to impact a family, a village, a city, a state, a nation and our world for Christ. Prayer is the avenue God has chosen to unleash His power to do His will.

....

So how do we begin to do this, with so much to pray for? However you pray is great as long as you pray using God's Word. The Holy Spirit will lead you. Romans 8:26-27 says, "In the same way the Spirit also helps our weakness; for we do not know how to pray as we should, but the Spirit Himself intercedes for us with groanings too deep for words; and He who searches the hearts knows what the mind of the Spirit is, because He intercedes for the saints according to the will of God."

In Acts 1:8, Jesus sent out His disciples throughout the world to be His witness. He continues to do so. And our prayers can go out to the outermost parts of the world.

What is our Jerusalem, Judea, Samaria, and remotest parts of the earth as we pray?

Our Jerusalem can be our homes, extended family, our church family, and local ministries.

Our Judea can be our neighborhood, our city, schools, and our state. Samaria can be our country including politicians, military, and whatever else impacts the country as a whole. Our remote parts of the earth can include missionaries and other countries.

I will give you an example of how I do this without feeling burdened. Each day I pray for my family using a scripture I have read or one that is on my heart. On different days I pray for the rest. For those who are saved, I pray often for protection and growth in the knowledge of God. They are standing in the front lines sharing the love of Christ, and our greatest gift to them is our prayers which are an eternal gift. And oh how our pastors and ministry leaders in and outside the church need us to take at least one day a week and intercede on their behalf.

For the unsaved, I pray that their "eyes will be opened," or may they hear the words of truth, the Gospel. Mark 12:30-31 commands, "'AND YOU SHALL LOVE THE LORD YOUR GOD WITH ALL YOUR HEART, AND WITH ALL YOUR SOUL, AND WITH ALL YOUR MIND, AND WITH ALL YOUR STRENGTH.' The second is this, 'YOU SHALL LOVE YOUR NEIGHBOR AS YOURSELF.' There is no other commandment greater than these." One of the greatest ways we can love others as we love ourselves is to pray for them.

May you take every complaint you have against someone and turn it into a prayer of blessing and stand amazed at what God will do in you and through you. Let us flood this land with our prayers and watch revival and spiritual awakening happen within and without our lands!

· · · · · · · · · · · · · · · · · · · Praise · · · · · · · · · · · · · · · · · · ·

For God so loved the world, that He gave His only begotten Son, that whoever believes in Him shall not perish, but have eternal life. For God did not send the Son into the world to judge the world, but that the world might be saved through Him.

JOHN 3:16-17

Confession

Lord, forgive me for not loving others as I love myself!
Forgive me for being quick to complain and slow to pray!

Thanksgiving

Thank You, Lord, for all the opportunities You are giving
me to be in Your presence as I pray for others. Thank You for
transforming me from the inside out as I pray for others and
for taking me from anger to joy and peace as I talk to You.

Intercession for Believers

For those who know You, Lord, I pray that their love may
abound still more and more in real knowledge and all
discernment, so that You may approve the things that are
excellent, in order to be sincere and blameless until the day
of Christ; having been filled with the fruit of righteousness
which comes through Jesus Christ, to Your glory and praise.

FROM PHILIPPIANS 1:9-11

Intercession for Those Who Don't Yet Believe

For those who don't know You, may they hear the message of
truth, the gospel of Your salvation and believe, so each one will
be marked in Christ with a seal, the promised Holy Spirit.

FROM EPHESIANS 1:13 NIV

· · · · · · · · · · · · · · · · · · · **Petition** · · · · · · · · · · · · · · · · · ·

Lord, help my love abound still more and more in real knowledge and all discernment, so that You may approve the things that are excellent, in order to be sincere and blameless until the day of Christ; having been filled with the fruit of righteousness which comes through Jesus Christ, to Your glory and praise.

FROM PHILIPPIANS 1:9-11

39

The Key to Remaining Unshaken and Empowered by Christ

.... Cyndie ....

We do not know what to do,
but our eyes are on you.

2 Chronicles 20:12 niv

As I was praying for my friend about her daughter's infuriating snag that was delaying her college graduation, the Lord led me to 2 Chronicles. I prayed these verses over the situation, and texted them to my friend. Unbeknownst to me, she was headed up to meet with the school at the very moment I was praying. God's timing is always amazing to me!

Since then, I've had many opportunities to cry out these verses to the Lord on behalf of my children, my husband, work, other family members, friends, and acquaintances. We might not have any idea what we should do, but if we keep our eyes on the Lord, despite the craziness swirling around us, then we can stand unshaken, empowered in Christ, knowing God will go before us and fight our battle for us. Our job is just to keep our eyes on the Lord and take each step of faith He has planned for us.

I love the story of King Jehoshaphat hidden in 2 Chronicles. The King of Judah finds out that he and his people will soon be under attack by not one, not two, but *three* armies. What I love is that his first response is not to stress out and run around crying or screaming. But he wasn't without emotion, either. Instead he took his concern right to the Lord.

2 Chronicles 20:3 says, "Alarmed, Jehoshaphat resolved to inquire of the Lord, and he proclaimed a fast for all Judah" (NIV). When everyone gathered to hear the king, he stood resolute before all of Judah. Can you imagine? And then, when he starts praying, he begins as we do in Moms in Prayer. He doesn't dive right into begging the Lord or pleading for protection. No, he started by praising God.

> The people of Judah came together to seek help from the Lord; indeed, they came from every town in Judah to seek him. Then Jehoshaphat stood up in the assembly of Judah and Jerusalem at the temple of the Lord in the front of the new courtyard and said:
>
> "Lord, the God of our ancestors, are you not the God who is in heaven? You rule over all the kingdoms of the nations. Power and might are in your hand, and no one can withstand you" (2 Chronicles 20:4-6 NIV).

After praising and thanking the Lord, Jehoshaphat cried out, "We have no power to face this vast army that is attacking us. We do not know what to do, but our eyes are on you" (verse 12 NIV).

Check out God's answer to the king—and to us. "Do not be afraid or discouraged because of this vast army. For the battle is not yours, but God's" (verse 15 NIV). Jehoshaphat and his comparatively small army are told, "You will not have to fight this battle. Take up your positions; stand firm and see the deliverance the Lord will give you, Judah and Jerusalem. Do not be afraid; do not be discouraged. Go out to face them tomorrow, and the Lord will be with you" (verse 17 NIV).

The first thing you might notice in 2 Chronicles 20 is that they are *not* worried or nervous, because they're keeping their focus on the Lord. Three big ol' armies are headed their way, and they're totally outnumbered. Yet, when the army gathered, they chose an unusual weapon to protect themselves: praise songs! "Jehoshaphat appointed men to sing to the LORD and to praise him for the splendor of his holiness as they went out at the head of the army" (verse 21 NIV).

How did they remain unshaken in the face of great calamity? They praised God! Now comes the completely amazing part. "As they began to sing and praise, the LORD set ambushes against the men of Ammon and Moab and Mount Seir who were invading Judah, and they were defeated" (verse 22 NIV). Rival armies began fighting each other, so much so that by the time Judah reached the battleground, this is what they saw: "When the men of Judah came to the place that overlooks the desert and looked toward the vast army, they saw only dead bodies lying on the ground; no one had escaped" (verse 24 NIV). In those days, the winning army took the plunder. And since there was no one else to claim the equipment, clothing, and expensive articles, God blessed His people with them.

When confronted with an overwhelming challenge, Jehoshaphat and his kingdom went to prayer instead of fear. By starting with praise, they moved their eyes off the problem and onto the ultimate Problem Solver. And though they didn't know what to do, they were unshaken, filled with God's inexplicable peace as they took those steps of faith.

What are you facing today? That battle is not yours: It's God's. Let Him empower you. Start by praising God for who He is, then rest in the fact that the Creator of the universe is going to take care of your problem.

· · · · · · · · · · · · · · · · · · Praise · · · · · · · · · · · · · · · · · ·

Lord, I praise You for Your power, that I need only to look to You, because You will go before me and fight my battles.

· · · · · · · · · · · · · · · · · Confession · · · · · · · · · · · · · · · · ·

Please forgive me for the times I take my eyes off You and become shaken and fearful.

·············· **Thanksgiving** ··············

I thank You Lord specifically for...

·············· **Intercession** ··············

I pray for _____ that he/she will keep his/her eyes on
You, even though _____ may not know what to do.

·············· **Petition** ··············

Lord, for myself, I do not know what to do in the area of
_____, but please help me keep my eyes on You, to
step out in faith, knowing that You will go before me.

40

Standing in the Gap

····················· Sally ·····················

*Night and day we pray earnestly for you, asking God
to let us see you again to fill the gaps in your faith.*

1 Thessalonians 3:10 nlt

*G*od has a mighty plan for this generation and the generations to follow. So we must be about prayer for this generation and the ones to come.

God is rising up an army of women who are praying for this next generation! This movement is called Moms in Prayer International. Our vision is that every school in the world will be covered with prayer.

What if you could change the world, not just for today but for decades to come? At Moms in Prayer International, we believe that a mom can be the single greatest force for good in the lives of her children and the children around her. We believe that lives and whole communities are changed forever when moms gather together to pray to the only One who can change a human heart. Moms can make the difference as they reach out to God in prayer—moms just like you or the one who raised you.

Our mission is simple: We impact children and schools worldwide for Christ by gathering women to pray. Our purpose, our whole reason for existing is...

- To pray that our children will receive Jesus as Lord and Savior, then stand boldly in their faith

- To pray for teachers and school staff
- To pray that teachers, school staff, and students come to faith in Jesus Christ
- To provide support and encouragement to moms who carry heavy burdens for their children
- To pray that our schools will be directed by biblical values and high moral standards
- To be an encouragement and a positive support to our schools

When you read Ezekiel 22, below, consider how this description sounds like today, here and now.

> "They have treated father and mother lightly within you. The alien they have oppressed in your midst; the father-less and the widow they have wronged in you. You have despised My holy things and profaned My sabbaths. Slanderous men have been in you for the purpose of shedding blood...One has committed abomination with his neighbor's wife and another has lewdly defiled his daughter-in-law. And another in you has humbled his sister, his father's daughter. In you they have taken bribes to shed blood; you have taken interest and prof-its, and you have injured your neighbors for gain by oppression, and you have forgotten Me," declares the Lord GOD (Ezekiel 22:7-12).

And God was about to deal with them!

> Can your heart endure, or can your hands be strong in the days that I will deal with you? I, the LORD, have spo-ken and will act. I will scatter you among the nations and I will disperse you through the lands, and I will consume your uncleanness from you. You will profane

yourself in the sight of the nations, and you will know
that I am the Lord (Ezekiel 22:14-16).

And yet God wanted to show mercy upon them!

> "I searched for a man among them who would build up
> the wall and stand in the gap before Me for the land, so
> that I would not destroy it; but I found no one. Thus I
> have poured out My indignation on them; I have con-
> sumed them with the fire of My wrath; their way I have
> brought upon their heads," declares the Lord God (Eze-
> kiel 22:30-31).

To stand in the gap is to stand between God and man and to pray
His mercy upon our land. I know God has an amazing plan for this
generation! As president of Moms in Prayer International, I am blessed
to get a bird's eye view of what God is doing around the world through
prayer.

God is rising up a generation like never before and we must be all
about praying for this next generation. We must "pray night and day,
earnestly for them, asking God to fill the gaps in their faith" (1 Thessalonians 3:10 nlt).

This generation is facing ungodly teachings, rumors of wars, natural disasters, terrorists, and much of a world that has turned its back
on God. And yet God is going to work through them powerfully. This
is a generation that can stand strong in the Lord if we will pray and
keep praying.

In the time of Moses, it seemed impossible for the children of Israel
to make it to the Promised Land. The children of God seemed to dis-
obey God one too many times. In Exodus 32 while Moses is with God,
the children are worshiping a golden calf! "The Lord said to Moses, 'I
have seen this people, and behold, they are an obstinate people. Now
then let Me alone, that My anger may burn against them and that I
may destroy them; and I will make of you a great nation'" (Exodus
32:9-10).

What does Moses do? He stands in the gap for the children of Israel!

"Then Moses entreated the LORD his God, and said, 'O LORD, why does Your anger burn against Your people whom You have brought out from the land of Egypt with great power and with a mighty hand?'" (Exodus 32:11).

Moses goes to intercessory prayer for them. And God hears and holds back judgment. Moses then leads God's people forward toward the promise land.

Nick Hall, founder of PULSE Movement and CEO of Mission America Coalition, has gathered together tens of thousands of college students to pray for our nation. He has witnessed their passion and wants others to know that this is a time for hope. He recently shared the good news via Instagram:

> There is a generation rising up that doesn't see boundaries and knows no limits. They are hungry for the things of God and ready to go. Bold. Fearless. Full of Faith. They aren't after a name as much as The Name and not after fame unless it is His. There is much hope for tomorrow... so don't let anyone tell you otherwise.

At Moms in Prayer, we work with many different ministries and leaders, like Nick, who remind us how important it is for us to never give up praying for the younger generations and to pay attention to how God is answering our prayers mightily.

Today many of the children we have prayed for have become pastors, missionaries, teachers, doctors, godly parents, leaders, politicians, athletes, and other professions. They are impacting our world for Christ.

I do webinars with many young ministry leaders, and their passion for Christ impassions me. I met with my youngest daughter's friends who recently graduated from college and are serving in a large church. The church is very smart as it has given them some leadership roles with the youth. God has raised them up to touch the next generation. As I heard their great love for Christ, I was stirred even greater to stand in the gap for them.

Several pastors around the world are helping to build up Moms in Prayer International in their country so the youth can be covered in prayer. They are opening up their churches for the women to gather, knowing this generation and the generation to come need our prayers.

Revival and spiritual awakening only come as we pray! God is waiting for us to stand in the gap so He can pour out His power to move powerfully in this generation and generations to come.

· · · · · · · · · · · · · · · · · **Praise** · · · · · · · · · · · · · · · · · ·

I will sing of Your lovingkindness forever and to all generations I will make known Your faithfulness. Your faithfulness continues through all generations and Your kingdom is an everlasting kingdom. Your dominion, Lord, endures throughout all generations!

FROM PSALM 89:1, PSALM 119:90, AND PSALM 145:13

· · · · · · · · · · · · · · · · **Confession** · · · · · · · · · · · · · · · · ·

Lord, forgive me when I forget the importance of intercessory prayer—of "standing in the gap" for others. Forgive me when I get complacent and forget to cry out to You on behalf of this next generation, that they will love You with their heart, mind, and soul, and love others as themselves.

· · · · · · · · · · · · · · · **Thanksgiving** · · · · · · · · · · · · · · · ·

I will cause Your name to be remembered in all generations; therefore the peoples will give You thanks forever and ever.

PSALM 45:17

Lord, thank You specifically for these things that I see You doing in this next generation for...

· · · · · · · · · · · · · · · · · Intercession · · · · · · · · · · · · · · · ·

*Lord, help _____ always remember to tell the next generation
the praises of the LORD, Your strength and Your wondrous
works that You have done. For You commanded us to teach
our children, that the generation to come might know, even
the children yet to be born, that they may arise and tell them
to their children, that they should put their confidence in You
and not forget Your works, but keep Your commandments.*

FROM PSALM 78:4-7

· · · · · · · · · · · · · · · · · Petition · · · · · · · · · · · · · · · · · ·

*Lord, help me to always remember to tell the next generation
the praises of the LORD, Your strength and Your wondrous
works that You have done. For You commanded us to teach
our children, that the generation to come might know, even
the children yet to be born, that they may arise and tell them
to their children, that they should put their confidence in You
and not forget Your works, but keep Your commandments.*

FROM PSALM 78:4-7

Moms in Prayer International

*I*f you're a mom, grandma, aunt, or woman concerned with the next generation, we encourage you to join a Moms in Prayer group. Praying the four steps of prayer—praise, silent confession, thanksgiving, and intercession—alongside another woman on behalf of your children is a powerful way to bring your burdens to the Lord. We have seen God transform lives in mighty ways as women come together to pray for children, their schools, and the school staff.

Moms in Prayer International was started in 1984 when Fern Nichols cried out to God to bring her at least one other mom to pray with her for her two eldest sons and their junior high school. God brought her more than just one other mom! With the help of Dr. James Dobson's radio broadcast, soon groups were starting all over the world, praying through the four steps on behalf of students and their schools. Moms in Prayer now has groups in every state around the USA and in 140-plus countries around the world. In 2015, Fern Nichols, the founder of Moms In Touch / Moms in Prayer International, passed the baton of leadership onto Sally Burke, who is now president of Moms in Prayer International.

Visit www.MomsInPrayer.org to see if there's a group near you. If not, the website offers all the resources you need to start a group. By registering your group online, your local Moms in Prayer leadership will offer you support as you begin. If you need additional assistance finding or starting a group, please contact info@MomsInPrayer.org or (855) 769-7729.

Everyone is welcome to sign up for our Scripture prayers, which are emailed Monday through Friday.

Sign up at www.MomsInPrayer.org.

About Sally Burke

Sally Burke, president of Moms in Prayer International, grew up in Cocoa Beach, Florida. As a girl, she was fascinated with the space program and later became a space shuttle engineer. It wasn't until after she married and gave birth to her first two children that she and her husband came to faith in Christ and God began changing her priorities. Her introduction to Moms in Prayer International in 1990 was life-changing. As a young mom and a new believer, she discovered how faithfully God works in kids' lives in answer to prayer. She also experienced the powerful bond of sisterhood among praying moms. Compelled by joy, Sally began to share this hope with other moms.

God has led her step by step, first as a Moms in Prayer group leader and then as a Moms in Prayer area coordinator for her hometown, Temecula, California, where God raised up 60 new Moms in Prayer groups. She later became the regional coordinator for all of Riverside County and its 25 school districts with 700 schools and half a million students. In 2008, Sally "took on the world" for Moms in Prayer International as the director of field ministry, providing spiritual and strategic direction to the ministry worldwide. During her tenure, God doubled the number of nations where Moms in Prayer groups are found.

Today, in her role as president of Moms in Prayer International, Sally is carrying on the legacy begun in 1984. The co-author of "Unshaken," Sally is a dynamic speaker and teacher who loves to encourage, equip, and empower women around the world in prayer. Sally has been interviewed on James Dobson's national radio program *Family Talk* as well as on *Today's Faith*, Calvary Chapel's national broadcast, and many other national and regional radio programs.

Sally and her husband, Ed, have four adult children—son Ryan married to Claire, daughter Ginae married to Garrett, son David married to Liz, and daughter Aubrie—and two grandchildren, Grant and Genevieve.

To contact Sally, email her at info@momsinprayer.org.

About Cyndie Claypool de Neve

*C*yndie Claypool de Neve, a former journalist who has an M.A. in Counseling Psychology, is the co-author of *When Moms Pray Together* published by Tyndale House in 2009, and *Unshaken* and *Unshaken Study Guide* published by Harvest House in 2017.

As the director of communications at Moms in Prayer International for five years, Cyndie launched the ministry's social media presence and the use of video storytelling. To encourage moms to pray daily, Cyndie coordinated the creation of the daily scripture prayers emailed to thousands of women every weekday morning. Cyndie also oversaw the organization's name change from Moms In Touch International to its current name, Moms in Prayer International, and helped establish the church-wide day of prayer, Bless Our Schools Sunday.

Today, she works as the senior director of creative and technical services at the megachurch Emmanuel Faith Community Church in Escondido, California. She leads a team of nine, overseeing communications, graphics, video, media, and IT.

Passionate about prayer and helping people find their God-given purpose, Cyndie enjoys speaking and teaching and has led many seminars, Bible studies, prayer groups, workshops, and Sunday school classes.

Cyndie and her husband, Marcel, live in Escondido, California, with their two creative children—Elliott and Zoe—and two rambunctious rescue dogs.

To contact Cyndie, visit www.cyndiedeneve.com.

Unshaken

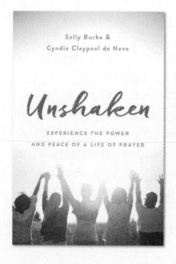

Your Faith Will Stand Unshaken When Your Prayers Shake Up the World

As you pray to the God of the universe, you're free to ask for the seemingly impossible. Align your heart with His will and pray with confidence, knowing He will answer according to His perfect plans and mighty power.

Join authors Sally Burke, president of Moms in Prayer International, and Cyndie Claypool de Neve on a quest to pray boldly in your daily struggles and difficult trials. When your strength is in short supply and your courage is battered, it's time to...

- discover the power of a biblical four-step prayer process that defeats fear

- read stories of women who experienced answered prayer in desperate circumstances

- learn how to pray for yourself and your loved ones in accordance with God's will

Your family and future are in secure hands when you release them to Jesus. And as you pray with firm faith, you'll see yourself and your world transformed.

Unshaken Study Guide and Personal Reflections

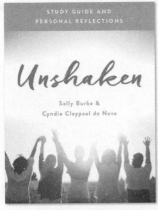

"I Keep My Eyes Always on the Lord. With Him at My Right Hand, I Will Not Be Shaken."
Psalm 16:8

You have every reason to pray with confidence when you're praying to the God of the universe in accordance with His perfect will. Learn how to pray boldly and consistently in this companion guide to *Unshaken* by Sally Burke, president of Moms in Prayer International, and Cyndie Claypool de Neve.

With provocative questions, recommended Scripture reading, and inspiring activities to complete, you'll discover fresh insights into prayer and be encouraged to entrust your family and future into the secure hands of Jesus.

Dig deep into this all-important study with a group or on your own, and get ready to see yourself and your world transformed.

To learn more about Harvest House books and
to read sample chapters, visit our website:

www.harvesthousepublishers.com

HARVEST HOUSE PUBLISHERS
EUGENE, OREGON